AI Literacy in K-16 Classrooms

Davy Tsz Kit Ng • Jac Ka Lok Leung
Maggie Jiahong Su • Iris Heung Yue Yim
Maggie Shen Qiao • Samuel Kai Wah Chu

AI Literacy in K-16 Classrooms

Davy Tsz Kit Ng
Faculty of Education
University of Hong Kong
Hong Kong, Hong Kong

Maggie Jiahong Su
Faculty of Education
University of Hong Kong
Hong Kong, Hong Kong

Maggie Shen Qiao
Faculty of Education
University of Hong Kong
Hong Kong, Hong Kong

Jac Ka Lok Leung
Division of Integrative Systems and Design
Hong Kong University of Science and
Technology
Hong Kong, China

Iris Heung Yue Yim
Faculty of Education
University of Hong Kong
Hong Kong, Hong Kong

Samuel Kai Wah Chu
Faculty of Education
University of Hong Kong
Hong Kong, Hong Kong

ISBN 978-3-031-18882-4   ISBN 978-3-031-18880-0   (eBook)
https://doi.org/10.1007/978-3-031-18880-0

This Springer imprint is published by the registered company Springer Nature Switzerland AG
The registered company address is: Gewerbestrasse 11, 6330 Cham, Switzerland

Foreword

Dear Readers,

There are many reasons why this book, *AI Literacy in K-16 Classrooms*, is so important to educators. First, AI is increasingly being used in schools and classrooms, and it is important for educators to understand how AI works and how it can be used to benefit students. Second, AI is changing the nature of work and learning, and educators need to be prepared to teach in a world where AI is playing an increasingly important role. Third, AI is raising ethical and social issues that educators need to be aware of and prepared to discuss with their students.

This book is essential reading for anyone who wants to understand AI and its implications for education.

AI tools are found in many aspects of our lives, and it is becoming increasingly difficult to remain ignorant about their implications on society. *AI Literacy in K-16 Classrooms* provides educators with the much-needed foundation to understand AI, its capabilities, and its potential implications in the classroom and beyond. Teachers are using AI tools to:

- Help grade essays
- Provide targeted feedback
- Offer personalized learning experiences
- And even teach classes

Students are using AI tools to:

- Get better grades
- Get more personalized feedback
- Have more customized learning experiences
- And even take classes

With these applications in mind, it is imperative that educators understand how AI works and how it can be used to benefit students. Teaching AI is essential reading for anyone who wants to understand AI and its implications for education.

If you want another reason why you should take the information and recommendations of this book to heart, consider this: most of this sentence and most of the preceding foreword text were written by a computer using an AI tool called GPT-3!

Beginning with a few simple prompting phrases, such as "Artificial Intelligence," "There are many reasons why this book is important to educators," and "Teachers are using AI tools to….," OpenAI's GPT-3 large language model (LLM) generated almost every word you see above. To arrive at the final text involved only a few minor edits to include the title of this book, and a few more prompts to suggest some alternative wordings and lists of AI tool uses.

There is no area of our lives, either as learners or educators, that is untouched by AI. Each and every subject, from art to zoology, now has a growing number of AI tools that generate new content or analyze and model the world around us. The era of ubiquitous AI has only just begun, making *AI Literacy in K-16 Education* a must-read for anyone who cares about the success of our education programs in preparing our students for the future.

Sincerely,

Prof. J. Stephen Downie
School of Information Science
University of Illinois, Urbana-Champaign

and

GPT-3
OpenAI Playground
https://beta.openai.com/playground

Foreword 2

Artificial intelligence (AI) technologies make our lives more efficient every day. These emerging technologies power many applications, programs, and services that help us do everyday things such as improving our online experience, enhancing our security, and increasing efficiency of our routine jobs. In the meantime, AI can cause us a lot of trouble due to privacy issues and human bias. Our students must learn about this emerging technology; hereby, AI education should be provided for all. This is supported by many AI education projects that have been launched around the world because AI topics conventionally are included in engineering faculty in higher education.

AI literacy is one of the important areas in educational research and practice. As one of the first AI education researchers, I am so happy to see this book *AI Literacy in K-16 Education* published. Professor Sam Chu and his team have expertise in literacy, technology education, and twenty-first century skills. In this book, they reviewed literature on AI education from kindergarten to tertiary level. They first define what AI literacy is, and discuss the landscape of AI education, followed by using various frameworks to describe AI literacy development. They continue to discuss instructional designs for the development at different educational levels. Finally, they raise this issue from teacher perspectives.

I believe this book would cater to different types of readers. If you are educators, you will gain more understanding of how to teach AI and assess student learning. If you are policy makers or curriculum designers, you will get inspired to design teacher professional programs or curriculum guidance. If you are AI developers, you will better understand what educational stakeholders need for developing AI content or learning applications. Finally, enjoy this book, and nurture our new generations with good AI literacy.

Thomas Kin Fung CHIU
Assistant Professor, Department of Curriculum and Instruction
The Chinese University of Hong Kong
Hong Kong, Hong Kong

About the Book

The book presents a review of the frameworks, content, pedagogies, and assessment of AI literacy education in supporting policymakers, educators, and parents to embed such an emerging area in the K-16 curriculum and into classrooms. Recommendations were proposed on how to develop AI literacy curricula and utilize age-appropriate technological tools and pedagogies to foster students' AI literacy skills or digital competencies. The book aims to provide an exhaustive summary of current evidence related to AI literacy with some highlighted cases. Some empirical studies were selected to illustrate how AI literacy models were applied in different countries and regions. The book captures the attention of multidisciplinary researchers looking for an overview of empirical studies that call for an AI literacy instructional design. The significance also lies in for all educators as a reference for practical methods. Finally, policymakers may borrow the models elicited in this book to reform education policies so as to design future-proof curricula and, most importantly, to prepare students with knowledge, mindsets, and dispositions conducive to dealing with future societal challenges.

Contents

Part I
Conceptualizing AI Literacy

Chapter 1
Introduction

Artificial intelligence (AI) is transforming across industries (e.g., marketing, science, art, education, entertainment) to facilitate people's living, learning, and working. According to the World Economic Forum's Future of Jobs Report (2020), 85 million jobs will be displaced by 2025, and, at the same time, 97 million new jobs will appear. People are accessing various types of AI-powered technologies daily (e.g., smart home appliances, smartphones, social media, chatbots). However, seldom do they know about the technologies or the algorithms behind, nor are they aware of potential ethical issues related to AI (e.g., privacy, surveillance, bias). As more age-appropriate curricula, resources, and tools are made available to learners, schools, and educators, AI literacy has emerged as a new digital competence that everyone should learn in response to this new era of intelligence. Different digital competence frameworks for educators (e.g., the ISTE, DigCompEdu standards) have included AI to update the latest educational standards to direct toward educators at all levels of education from early childhood to higher education (ISTE, 2022; Riina et al., 2022). With the exponential pace of technological advancement, AI literacy will soon become one of the most important twenty-first century technological literacy that everyone should learn in our digitizing world (Ng et al., 2021a, b).

This book conceptualizes the term AI literacy, illustrates the proposed conceptual frameworks of AI literacy education, explores how AI literacy is taught across countries/regions, and discusses a range of pedagogical approaches, content, and technological and assessment tools that leverage K–16 students' understandings and motivational capacity. This book is written for researchers, educators, policymakers, parents, and AI professionals who wish to foster an evolving set of AI skills and knowledge for their target learners. The goal is to prepare learners for an uncharted future with drastic technological changes. Readers will find a spectrum of theoretical and pragmatic discussions on AI literacy education. The discussions will be covered by K–16 educational levels as well as stories from different parts of the world. The book presents a review of AI literacy education which includes practical recommendations to develop age-appropriate AI literacy curricula, technological

D. T. K. Ng et al., *AI Literacy in K-16 Classrooms*,
https://doi.org/10.1007/978-3-031-18880-0_1

tools, pedagogies, and assessments. In Part III, a framework of AI literacy is developed based on the P21's Framework for the 21st Century Learning (2009) that not only focuses on technical skills but also details on how AI technologies can be used to enhance and innovate education and training.

1.1 Key Inquiry Questions

AI education first started in university computer science education which required advanced programming competencies that were not designed for K–12 and non-computer science students. Over the last two decades, most of the learners who would study or required to take AI courses are from computer science backgrounds who design robotics and software, construct models, and handle data structures (McCarthy, 2007; Wong et al., 2020). As might be expected, educators face challenges in coming up with a sound approach in scaffolding K–12 children and non-computer science undergraduates with these technical concepts and skills in the early 2010s. However, with the breakthroughs in AI learning technologies and substantial demand for AI skills across industries, teaching AI is no longer as difficult as it was in the past. Furthermore, the increase in accessibility to a wide range of AI technologies, such as data analytics tools, intelligent agents, chatbots, and writing assistants, also make sense for learners to understand, use, and communicate with AI to facilitate their living, learning, and working. However, in schools, teachers and students are novel to these subjects, and they may not be ready to adapt to such digital transformation. To overcome these challenges, there is an urgent need to support capacity building for all teachers and students to leverage digital technologies across the world.

Nowadays, university faculty have designed learning programs to equip non-computer science undergraduates with AI digital competencies for future workforce (Kong et al., 2021). In K–12 education, the current uses and impact of AI have spurred a demand to create a global consensus on how to equip young learners with the competencies needed to understand the technology and its related ethical dilemmas (UNESCO, 2022). According to the UNESCO (2022)'s report, 11 countries have developed and endorsed official curricula to grow up the next generation to become responsible citizens for success in today's digital world. Overall, all K–16 learners need to be equipped with a level of AI competencies. These include knowledge, skills, values, and attitudes to become so-called AI literate, which is becoming a new learning standard of our century.

On this note, this book introduces an exploratory review that helps conceptualize the newly emerging concept "AI literacy," in search for a sound theoretical foundation to define, teach, and evaluate AI literacy. Grounded in literature on existing peer-reviewed articles in renowned databases including Web of Science and Scopus, this book proposed a set of important concepts to foster learners AI literacy based on the adaptation of classic literacies based on content and systematic analysis. This book sheds light on the consolidated definition, teaching, and ethical concerns on AI literacy, establishing the groundwork for future research such as competency development and assessment criteria on AI literacy.

While the development of students' AI literacy skills has become a potential technological skill as part of their education similar to digital literacy (which will be further discussed in later chapters), researchers have directed their efforts in examining different learning artifacts and innovative pedagogical approaches that may facilitate the acquisition of these knowledge and skills among students (Chai et al., 2020; Wong et al., 2020). All in all, a few fundamental questions will be addressed in this book:

- *How do researchers define the term "AI literacy"?*
- *How do educators help learners develop AI literacy in aspects of learning artifacts, pedagogical approaches, and subject matters?*
- *How do researchers evaluate students' AI literacy skills?*
- *What are the ethical and human-centered considerations in the domain of AI literacy?*
- *How should we prepare teachers to foster students' AI competency?*

1.2   Organization

The organization of this book was inspired by the authors' experiences in implementing AI literacy education. Many schools may have initialized the incorporation of AI into their curriculum and classrooms already; however, we find that many educators feel anxious that they are not well prepared for the implementation of AI curricula as it is a relatively new form of education. In fact, the first author has heard technology companies developing AI-based products and teaching tools too abruptly without considering teachers' and students' needs. This opens up risks of wasting manpower and resources if these products are not based on pedagogical grounds and justified theoretical frameworks. Therefore, the book is structured in a way that readers will first understand the importance of AI literacy and then be introduced to guidelines and methods that can help students to develop such AI skills in a more gradual, humanistic, and systematic manner.

The book is divided into three parts. Part I focuses on a higher conceptual level of AI literacy, putting forward notions that try to encapsulate a variety of education contexts, foregrounding the emergence and urgency for educators and learners to embrace the era of AI. Part II travels deep in reviewing the efforts by scholars around the round across different educational levels, presenting scoping reviews that guide K–16 educators to develop their pedagogy, content, technology and assessments for their students. Part III proposes our vision of AI literacy. We have identified digital competences that AI developers and educators should take into account when devising learning tools, platforms, lesson plans, and assignments in order to help reinforce students' acquisition of AI literacy skills. Our suggestions on how to provide effective scaffolding support to their students is provided. Overall, this book aims to serve as an introduction and reference of resources for our educators, colleagues, and peers to update the evolution of this area, such that we can take part in designing effective and exciting learning experiences for our learners.

Part I (Chaps. 2, 3, and 4): Conceptualizing AI Literacy
The development of the concepts on AI literacy education is introduced and discussed. To begin with, readers may feel confused about the differences and similarities between AI literacy and AI education (AIED). Chapter 2 first has a quick glance at historical perspectives of AI and further looks into conceptual differences between the two jargons. Chapter 3 discusses reasons why all learners from kindergarten to higher education should learn AI. Chapter 4 examines how AI literacy is adapted from other digital literacies and presents an overview of AI literacy, helping readers to understand what is entailed in it and what we learn about it through existing research. An analysis on curriculum around the world is conducted to let readers appreciate the efforts by current educators that helped students acquire these literacies.

Part II (Chaps. 5, 6, 7, and 8): AI Literacy in K–16 Education
Readers will be introduced to the existing research findings about the pedagogy, content knowledge, learning artifacts, and assessment for K–16 students in association to the development of twenty-first century skills. An exploratory review summary on the AI literacy education from K–12 to higher education will be provided. Chapters 4, 5, 6, 7, and 8 use content and thematic analysis to understand how AI literacy education is implemented across different levels of study. A range of teaching strategies are recommended to foster students' acquisition of AI literacy skills.

Part III (Chaps. 9, 10, and 11): AI Literacy for Instructional Designers
In the last part of this book, we provide guidelines to developers, researchers, and education practitioners who plan to develop AI literacy instructional designs for students. Chapter 9 addresses the importance of human-centered considerations for AI developers to design tools and platforms that place users at the center. Chapter 10 taps into how teachers can be trained up with necessary skills, knowledge, and techniques for AI literacy education. The chapter will also propose a set of twenty-first century skills standards for educators to devise lesson plans, activities, and assignments to help reinforce students' acquisition of AI literacy skills. Moreover, teachers will find helpful recommendations on how to provide proper and effective scaffolding support to their students. Finally, the concluding Chap. 11 links back to the basic premises we set up in this introduction to add AI literacy as part of the twenty-first century skills. This aims to lay out guidelines and suggestions for AI literacy implementation, using the P21's Framework for the 21st Century Learning (2009).

References

Chai, C. S., Rahmawati, Y., & Jong, M. S. Y. (2020). Indonesian science, mathematics, and engineering preservice teachers' experiences in STEM-TPACK design-based learning. *Sustainability, 12*(21), 9050.

ISTE. (2022). *Artificial intelligence in education. Putting educators and students in the driver's Seat.* Retrieved from https://www.iste.org/areas-of-focus/AI-in-education

Kong, S. C., Cheung, W. M. Y., & Zhang, G. (2021). Evaluation of an artificial intelligence literacy course for university students with diverse study backgrounds. *Computers and Education: Artificial Intelligence, 2*, 100026.

McCarthy, J. (2007). From here to human-level AI. *Artificial Intelligence, 171*(18), 1174–1182.

Ng, D. T. K., Leung, J. K. L., Chu, S. K. W., & Qiao, M. S. (2021a). AI literacy: Definition, teaching, evaluation and ethical issues. *Proceedings of the Association for Information Science and Technology, 58*(1), 504–509.

Ng, D. T. K., Leung, J. K. L., Chu, S. K. W., & Qiao, M. S. (2021b). Conceptualizing AI literacy: An exploratory review. *Computers and Education: Artificial Intelligence, 2*, 100041.

Riina, V., Stefano, K., & Yves, P. (2022). *DigComp 2.2: The Digital Competence Framework for Citizens – With new examples of knowledge, skills and attitudes.* Retrieved from https://publications.jrc.ec.europa.eu/repository/handle/JRC128415

Silva, E. (2009). Measuring skills for 21st-century learning. *Phi delta kappan, 90*(9), 630–634.

UNESCO. (2022). *K-12 AI Curricula: A mapping of government-endorsed AI curricula.* Retrieved from https://unesdoc.unesco.org/ark:/48223/pf0000380602

Wong, G. K., Ma, X., Dillenbourg, P., & Huan, J. (2020). Broadening artificial intelligence education in K-12: Where to start? *ACM Inroads, 11*(1), 20–29.

World Economic Forum. (2020). *The Future of Jobs Report 2020.* Retrieved from https://www3.weforum.org/docs/WEF_Future_of_Jobs_2020.pdf

Chapter 2
AI Education and AI Literacy

Our twenty-first century is characterized by its rapid technological advancement. Our lifestyle and ways of interacting with people have changed significantly compared to around a decade ago in the early 2010s as AI technologies turn ubiquitous across industries and in our everyday lives. Artificial intelligence has spread across industries to enhance our living, learning, and working experience with exciting technological innovations such as computer vision, natural language processing, robotics and motion, machine and deep learning, and neural networks (Chen et al., 2022; Dong et al., 2021; Zawacki-Richter et al., 2019). Applications of AI have become in many parts of our everyday life (e.g., smart home appliances, smartphones, chatbots, search engines). In the field of education, schools began to use AI-enabled technologies to leverage students' personalized learning and reduce teachers' administrative work, thus offering more learning support and interactive learner experience (Roll & Wylie, 2016). Therefore, a field has gradually taken shape over the last few decades – AI in education (AIED).

Vast majority of the public acknowledges the existence of AI services and devices, but seldom do students know about the concepts and technology behind or aware of potential ethical issues related to AI (Burgsteiner et al., 2016; Ghallab, 2019). In recent years, AI has become essential skills to play critical roles across disciplines and industries (Ng et al., 2021; Touretzky et al., 2019). Students need to learn how to use AI technologies wisely, as well as to discriminate between ethical and unethical actions (Rodríguez-García et al., 2021). This gives rise to an emerging term "AI literacy" that drives the need that everyone should learn the basic AI knowledge and skills behind these technologies. However, many may feel confused about the similarities and differences between AI education and AI literacy. Before looking into the two jargons, this chapter first has a quick glance at what AI is from a historical perspective and further looks deeper into the conceptual differences between AIED and AI literacy education.

2.1 A Historical Perspective

Artificial intelligence was first introduced as "the science and engineering of making intelligent machines in 1956" (McCarthy, 2007, p. 2). At that time, Newell and Simon (1956) invented a "thinking machine" that was considered as the first computer program that simulated human intelligence to solve complex problems. This idea advanced our understanding of how humans think and make basic contributions to artificial intelligence and the psychology of human cognition. At the beginning, AI was used to handle limited tasks (e.g., automation, chess playing). Researchers called it the rule-based AI that people use programs and algorithms to reason and solve problems based on predetermined rules and environment (McCarthy, 2007). In today's era of rapid technological advancement and exponential increases in large datasets known as "big data," AI has transitioned to everyday applications on an unprecedented scale. The large datasets in near real-time enables people to drive autonomously, view videos and media posts based on recommendations (e.g., Netflix, YouTube, Facebook), do shopping online according to AI-based advertisements, and detect frauds to enhance working efficiency. We can see that AI has been broadened to perform a wide range of complex tasks with the exciting innovations (Zawacki-Richter et al., 2019).

Artificial intelligence refers to computerized machines and systems that mimic human intelligence to facilitate people to conduct various tasks and solve complex problems (Wang, 2019). However, there are quite a few ambiguous buzzwords about subfields of AI such as machine learning, deep learning, and neural networks which sometimes may be confusing. Here we provide some basic definitions to describe the relationship of these buzzwords to AI. First, machine learning (ML) exhibits the experiential "learning" associated with human intelligence which has the capacity to learn and improve its analyses through computational algorithms (Helm et al., 2020). These algorithms use large datasets to recognize patterns and effectively "learn" in order to train the machines and models to conduct various tasks (e.g., make autonomous recommendations, decisions). After sufficient repetitions and algorithm refinement, the machine becomes more ready for people to input datasets to predict an outcome. Throughout the processes, people can compare the outcomes with a set of desired outcomes in order to judge the accuracy of the algorithm to iteratively perfect the AI's capability to predict future outcomes (Helm et al., 2020).

Deep learning and neural networks are more complex versions of these models that make use of hierarchical layers to generate the final outputs. The network first begins with an input layer that then progressly involves a number of "hidden layers" that responds to different features (e.g., age, gender, ethnicity). These middle layers allow the AI-empowered model to enhance its understanding as the inputs ascend "deeper," without explicitly programmed directions. The model conducts specific actions on multiple layers and further successively improves its accuracy as new data is available. Since the model is similar to the way the human brain functions, the model is called "neural networks" and thus gives rise to a new form of AI, known as "deep learning."

In the educational field, AI could automate administrative processes, enhance learning experiences, and facilitate students' interactions. Using artificial intelligence in education (AIED) has emerged as a research field since the 1980s, as marked by the first publication of the International Journal of Artificial Intelligence in Education in 1989 and the formation of the International AI in Education Society in 1993 (Pinkwart, 2016). Researchers and educators have contributed to AI technologies in educational developments to design AI-driven tools for learning such as intelligent tutoring systems, recommendation systems, computational linguistics, and intelligent agents and use AI to understand, assess, and improve students' learning (Alkhatlan & Kalita, 2018; Chen et al., 2020; Hwang et al., 2020; Williamson & Eynon, 2020). AIED applications have been employed to facilitate teaching, learning, and administration through data mining, learning analytics, and learning intelligent agents in educational contexts (Chen et al., 2020; Hwang et al., 2020).

Since then, AI has affected many facets of human life rather than merely computer industries, which drive the need that everyone should learn AI (Ng et al., 2021). Over the past two decades, AI was conventionally taught at tertiary level as a field of computer science education (Chiu, 2021). Teaching AI stemmed from the invention of some programming languages (e.g., BASIC, LOGO, Prolog) by Seymour Papert in the 1980s. In 1995, Stuart Russell and Peter Norvig published an authoritative AI textbook that was widely used for over 1500 schools across the world. The book listed five major categories of AI concepts that were taught at the undergraduate level: (1) problem-solving strategies, (2) knowledge, reasoning and planning, (3) uncertain knowledge and reasoning, (4) machine learning, and (5) communication, perceiving, and acting. There were few mentions in literature where children were encouraged to conduct AI projects in playful environments to learn computational concepts (e.g., variables, recursion, representations, process) (Kahn & Carlsson, 1985). However, without age-appropriate curricula and teaching tools, educators faced difficulties in scaffolding young learners to visualize the complex AI concepts (Wong et al., 2020; Ng et al., 2021). Introducing K–12 students to AI has been impossible and sporadic. Until 2019, the emergence of developmentally appropriate curriculum and technologies has made AI teaching possible for younger learners to develop their AI competencies to become a responsible digital citizen and get ready for the future workplace. Since then, scholars in K–16 education discuss how to incorporate AI into their classrooms and started to design frameworks, measurements, models, and reviews in K–16 AI literacy education (Druga et al., 2019; Long & Magerko, 2020; Ng et al., 2021; Touretzky et al., 2019).

2.2   AI Education Versus AI Literacy

2.2.1   Artificial Intelligence in Education

Artificial intelligence in education (AIED) refers to the use of AI technologies and application programs which serve as intelligent tutors, tutees, tools/ partners, and policymaking advisors in educational settings to facilitate teaching, learning, and decision making (Hwang et al., 2020). These tools simulate human intelligence to "make inferences, judgments, or predictions, computer systems can provide personalized guidance, support, or feedback to students" (Hwang et al., 2020, p. 1). Research on AIED involves diverse research focused on different AI technologies. For example, Hwang et al. (2020) used fuzzy expert systems to take into account both the affective and cognitive status of students so as to improve their learning achievement and reduce their anxiety in a fifth-grade mathematics course. Chih-Ming and Ying-You (2020) developed a computer-mediated communication competence forecasting model to predict communication behavior and objectives during collaborative problem-based learning. Baker et al. (2021) analyzed how learning analytics is being methodologically influenced by recent trends in the fields of educational data mining, quantitative ethnography, and learning at scale to increase impact on policy and practice (Baker et al., 2021). Okonkwo and Ade-Ibijola (2021) investigated the benefits and challenges of educational chatbots, as well as future research areas such as providing personalized services for institutional employees and students.

With the increasing amount of AIED research articles being published, it is necessary to systematically review the relevant issues. Hinojo-Lucena et al. (2019) conducted a bibliometric analysis of 132 articles on AI in higher education to investigate the relationship between the number of authors and papers and to explore the main source titles, organizations, authors, and countries about AI in higher education. Roll and Wylie (2016) reviewed 47 articles from 1994, 2004, and 2014 in the journal of AIED to explore the research foci in the field of AIED. However, Chen et al. (2020) believed that findings may not provide an essential understanding of the research since only a single article is considered and there are no studies reviewed after 2014. Zawacki-Richter et al. (2019) analyzed 146 articles regarding the AIED applications in higher education and figured out 4 major areas of AIED applications: profiling and prediction, intelligent tutoring systems, assessment and evaluation, and adaptive learning systems. Although bibliometric analysis is principally useful in analyzing sizable literature data, an in-depth investigation by using a systematic review methodology is needed (Chen et al., 2020).

Recent reviews contributed to look at the major research issues and AI technologies adopted in highly cited AIED studies and proposed a theoretical framework for this field. For example, Chen et al. (2020) reviewed 30 articles from Web of Science and Google Scholar with keywords "AI" and "Education" and identified that AI has taken the form of digital technologies such as automated assessment, adaptive learning, humanoid robots, and web-based chatbots to perform teachers' duties, facilitate administrative functions, and review students' assignments effectively to achieve higher quality in education. Some systems used AI technologies such as machine learning and natural language processing (NLP) to personalize students' needs to foster learning engagement and improve students' performance (Chen et al., 2020). Chen et al. (2020) conducted a systematic review using 45 highly cited AIED articles indexed in Web of Science and Scopus databases from 1990 to 2016 to identify the application and theory gaps during the rise of AI in education. It is indicated that there was a rising interest in and impact of AIED research over the past two decades. It is found that deep learning technologies (e.g., neural networks, NLP, biomedical detection) have great potential to be used in the educational fields for future studies and employ these AI technologies and engage deeply with educational theories. All these reviews emphasize on how educators use AI technologies to enhance learning and teaching and facilitate administration. These AIED research reviews focus on using AI technologies for educational purposes, and none of the reviews discovered how to teach and learn AI and related computer science concepts. All of the reviews exclude computer science, AI and machine learning related courses learning, learning technologies to learn AI and teaching methods, and computational thinking related studies (Chen et al., 2020).

2.2.2   Artificial Intelligence Literacy

Artificial intelligence literacy studies encompass efforts toward equipping learners with literacy skills to thrive in an AI-saturated future (Wang & Cheng, 2021). In earlier years of publication, AI learning was only instituted in computer science education in higher education which required advanced programming competencies, while it was not at an appropriate level for K–12 learners. Many pioneers in higher education gravitated toward the use of robotics making (Klassner, 2002; Imberman, 2004), software development (Mota-Valtierra et al., 2019; Estevez et al., 2019), and game design through syntax-based programming (Wallace et al., 2010; Wong et al., 2020). These pedagogies have demonstrated the potential to improve computer science students' AI learning motivation (Wallace et al., 2010) and knowledge acquisition (McGovern & Fager, 2007). However, K–12 educators faced challenges in scaffolding students to understand AI concepts due to technical complexity which make teaching AI difficult to become part of K–12 education (e.g., McCarthy, 2007; Steinbauer et al., 2021; Wong et al., 2020). With the emergence of age-appropriate technologies such as Blockly-based programming (Estevez et al., 2019), simulation, and robotics (Narahara & Kobayashi, 2018), AI becomes possible for learners to program applications that involve AI elements without mastering the complex syntax of programming languages and algorithms. This raises the learning possibilities to consider AI education as part of ICT and STEM education curriculum.

With the breakthroughs of emerging AI learning artifacts, teaching AI is not as difficult as it was in the past. Educators began engaging non-computer science undergraduates, as well as primary and secondary school students in AI learning (Chiu, 2021; Xia et al., 2022). Studies have shown a positive interplay between artificial and human intelligence that nontechnical students could also gain interests and fundamental understandings of AI in interdisciplinary and liberal arts curricula (Cicirello, 2008; Lichtenthaler, 2018). In primary and secondary education, researchers have drawn attention to age-appropriate technological tools to scaffold students' AI understanding with well-designed Blockly programming interfaces such as Scratch and simple machine learning model builders that could allow learners to access the speech and object recognition (Garcia et al., 2019; Toivonen et al., 2020). These advances create opportunities for educators to adopt effective pedagogical approaches with these tools to foster students' AI literacy and appreciation of the five "big ideas" of AI (Touretzky et al., 2019). As such, all students should receive a solid foundation for their studies at their young ages to prepare their future career in the era of AI, thereby encouraging nontechnical university students, as well as primary and secondary students to learn how to use AI and its underlying concepts and related AI-enhanced soft skills including teamwork, organization, social awareness, and ethical concerns (e.g., Carpio Cañada et al., 2015; Sabuncuoglu, 2020).

Recent AI-related technologies such as smart devices, search engines, chatbots, and computer games have become common in our daily life. Most people know about the existence of these services and products, but only a few understand the technology and principles behind them (Ng et al., 2021). With more age-appropriate technologies, scholars began to focus on the learning and teaching of AI knowledge and technology and the need to use AI ethically to solve real-life problems for younger learners. For example, Burgsteiner et al. (2016) believed that the younger generation should learn about AI knowledge and technologies (e.g., basic concepts of algorithms, data structures, and programs). Another study Lin and Van Brummelen (2021) developed an AI curriculum to test students' motivation (e.g., intrinsic motivation, career interest, confidence to use AI, and learning satisfaction) among 420 primary students in China. These studies provide evidence on adopting digital technologies to learn AI via well-defined curricula and activities. However, the learning design and related utilities of AI learning artifacts in primary and secondary classrooms have only recently been explored (Chiu & Chai, 2020; Toivonen et al., 2020). To date, no holistic guidelines and reviews of teaching AI have existed.

2.2.3   Similarities and Differences Between AIED and AI Literacy

Now let's clarify the similarities and differences between AIED and AI literacy. First, AI technologies provide great potential for students to facilitate their learning. However, these technologies may be novel to students and are not familiar with them. Therefore, educators have the role to help develop students' technological knowledge and skills in order to use the tools ethically and wisely. Recently, scholars suggested the need to update students' digital competence to facilitate their learning and working (Rina et al., 2022; Zhang & Aslan, 2021).

Studies have explored the digital competencies to incorporate AI into classrooms (e.g., ISTE, 2022; Celik, 2022). We can see that AIED and AI literacy may share common ideas (e.g., digital competence to use AI applications effectively, using AI to express a knowledge domain, communicating with peers using AI, using AI applications ethically). However, AI literacy research studies focus more on how to learn and teach AI, instead of understanding the adoption of AI techniques for educational purposes. Second, AIED identifies how to use computers to perform cognitive tasks that are usually associated with human minds, including using AI technology to facilitate learning and teaching in different subjects such as language

- **Use AI to facilitate people's learning**
- **Use AI to learn a knowledge domain (e.g., language, math)**
- **Communicate and collaborate effectively with AI**

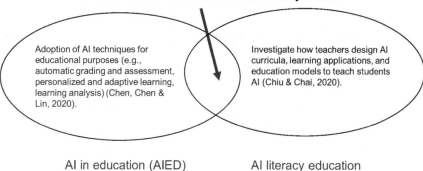

Adoption of AI techniques for educational purposes (e.g., automatic grading and assessment, personalized and adaptive learning, learning analysis) (Chen, Chen & Lin, 2020).

Investigate how teachers design AI curricula, learning applications, and education models to teach students AI (Chiu & Chai, 2020).

AI in education (AIED)   AI literacy education

Fig. 2.1 Similarities and differences between AIED and AI literacy education

(Liang et al., 2021), nursing (Hwang et al., 2020), and mathematics education (Hwang & Tu, 2021). However, AI literacy focuses on the design and implementation of AI curricula, learning applications, and pedagogical models in K–16 education that aims to develop students' AI knowledge, skills, and attitudes (Rina et al., 2022). Third, AI literacy is not inclusive of examining how AI technology facilitates governments, schools, and educators to improve policy settings and educational administration. From the above arguments, we believe that AI literacy (learning about AI) should be different from AIED (learning with AI applications and from AI-driven systems).

Without a universal consensus of these terms, some may identify AI literacy as a subset of AI education (Wang & Cheng, 2021). Some studies use AI education to describe AI curriculum, pedagogy, and activities and do not indicate the differences between the two terms (Chiu & Chai, 2020; Yau et al., 2022). Furthermore, in terms of learning artifacts, we argue that for AI literacy education, it is not a must to use AI technologies to learn AI concepts. Prior studies suggested the use of non-AI artifacts, low-technology settings, and unplugged activities such as digital storytelling, role-play, and social media tools to scaffold students' AI understandings (Julie et al., 2020; Ng & Chu, 2021; Rodríguez-García et al., 2021). To visualize our standpoint, the differences between AIED and AI literacy is summarized in with sample studies in Fig. 2.1 and Table 2.1.

2.3 Conclusion

The term "AI literacy" was first coined by Burgsteiner et al. (2016) and Kandlhofer et al. (2016) who proposed it as the ability to understand the knowledge and concepts behind these AI-driven technologies. On top of knowing and using AI

Table 2.1 Differences and similarities between AIED and AI literacy

	AI in education (AIED)	AI literacy
Research focus	Identify how to use computers to perform cognitive tasks that are usually associated with human minds, particularly learning and problem-solving in instruction, teaching and administration (Chen et al., 2020) Understand and improve the adoption of AI techniques for educational purposes (e.g., automatic grading and assessment, personalized and adaptive learning, learning analysis) (Chen et al., 2020)	Investigate how teachers design AI curricula, learning applications, and education models to teach students AI (Chiu & Chai, 2020) Examine how students develop AI understandings affectively, behaviorally, and cognitively (e.g., perceived ability, motivation, career interest, confidence to use AI, learning satisfaction) (Chen et al., 2022; Ng & Chu, 2021) Emphasize the learning and teaching of AI knowledge and technology, and the need to use AI ethically (Chen et al., 2020)
Research methods	Qualitative and quantitative methods to examine how governments, educational institutes, educators, and students use AI technology to enhance learning and teaching and facilitate administration and policy setting	Qualitative and quantitative methods to examine how students develop AI and related computer science concepts via AI curricula and activities
Learning tools/ artifacts	AI technology (e.g., NLP chatbot, adaptive systems, intelligent agents)	AI and related digital technology (e.g., simulation of neural networks, robotic coding, games) Non-AI artifacts (e.g., gamified elements, story writing, role-play)
Sample research	Use intelligent agent systems to improve students' learning (Hwang et al., 2020) Develop a computer-mediated communication competence forecasting model to facilitate collaborative problem-based learning (Chih-Ming & Ying-You, 2020) Adopt learning analytics and educational data mining to increase impact on policy and practice (Baker et al., 2021) Use chatbots to provide personalized services for institutional employees and students (Okonkwo & Ade-Ibijola, 2021)	Motivate students to learn AI via social media tools, gamification, and simulation tasks (Ng & Chu, 2021) Enhance students' intrinsic motivation, career interest, confidence to use AI, and learning satisfaction through an AI curriculum (Lin & Van Brummelen, 2021) Understand how students learn AI concepts with digital technologies in different pedagogical approaches (Wong et al., 2020) Develop students' AI literacy and ethical awareness via AI curricula and framework (Burgsteiner et al., 2016; Kandlhofer et al., 2016)
Similarities	Use AI-driven technologies to learn different subject knowledge Foster students' digital (AI) literacy to use different AI technologies to facilitate their learning Enhance students to communicate, collaborate, and use AI effectively for learning purposes	

ethically, it serves as a set of competencies that enable people to critically evaluate AI technologies, communicate, and collaborate effectively with AI (Long & Magerko, 2020). After knowing the differences between AIED and AI literacy, the conceptualized term "AI literacy" can provide a strong foundation for future research (Druga et al., 2019; Long & Magerko, 2020) and enabled further examination of better instructional design that fosters AI literacy (Chai et al., 2021). This next section will discuss the reasons why K–16 students should learn AI literacy.

References

Alkhatlan, A., & Kalita, J. (2018). Intelligent tutoring systems: A comprehensive historical survey with recent developments. *arXiv preprint arXiv:1812.09628*.

Baker, R. S., McLaren, B. M., Hutt, S., Richey, J. E., Rowe, E., Almeda, M., ... & Andres, J. M. (2021, June). Towards sharing student models across learning systems. In *International Conference on Artificial Intelligence in Education* (pp. 60–65). Springer.

Burgsteiner, H., Kandlhofer, M., & Steinbauer, G. (2016, March). Irobot: Teaching the basics of artificial intelligence in high schools. In *Proceedings of the AAAI Conference on Artificial Intelligence* (Vol. 30, No. 1).

Carpio Cañada, J., Mateo Sanguino, T. J., Merelo Guervós, J. J., & Rivas Santos, V. M. (2015). Open classroom: Enhancing student achievement on artificial intelligence through an international online competition. *Journal of Computer Assisted Learning, 31*(1), 14–31.

Celik, I. (2022). Towards intelligent-TPACK: An empirical study on teachers' professional knowledge to ethically integrate artificial intelligence (AI)-based tools into education. *Computers in Human Behavior, 138*, 107468.

Chai, C. S., Lin, P. Y., Jong, M. S. Y., Dai, Y., Chiu, T. K., & Qin, J. (2021). Perceptions of and behavioral intentions towards learning artificial intelligence in primary school students. *Educational Technology & Society, 24*(3), 89–101.

Chen, L., Chen, P., & Lin, Z. (2020). Artificial intelligence in education: A review. *IEEE Access, 8*, 75264–75278.

Chen, X., Zou, D., Xie, H., Cheng, G., & Liu, C. (2022). Two decades of artificial intelligence in education. *Educational Technology & Society, 25*(1), 28–47.

Chih-Ming, C., & Ying-You, L. (2020). Developing a computer-mediated communication competence forecasting model based on learning behavior features. *Computers and Education: Artificial Intelligence, 1*, 100004.

Chiu, T. K. (2021). A holistic approach to the design of artificial intelligence (AI) education for K-12 schools. *TechTrends, 65*(5), 796–807.

Chiu, T. K., & Chai, C. S. (2020). Sustainable curriculum planning for artificial intelligence education: A self-determination theory perspective. *Sustainability, 12*(14), 5568.

Cicirello, V. A. (2008). An interdisciplinary course on artificial intelligence designed for a liberal arts curriculum. *Journal of Computing Sciences in Colleges, 23*(3), 120–127.

Dong, S., Wang, P., & Abbas, K. (2021). A survey on deep learning and its applications. *Computer Science Review, 40*, 100379.

Druga, S., Vu, S. T., Likhith, E., & Qiu, T. (2019). Inclusive AI literacy for kids around the world. In *Proceedings of FabLearn 2019* (pp. 104–111).

Estevez, J., Garate, G., & Graña, M. (2019). Gentle introduction to artificial intelligence for high-school students using scratch. *IEEE Access, 7*, 179027–179036.

Garcia, N. C., Morerio, P., & Murino, V. (2019). Learning with privileged information via adversarial discriminative modality distillation. *IEEE Transactions on Pattern Analysis and Machine Intelligence, 42*(10), 2581–2593.

Ghallab, M. (2019). Responsible AI: Requirements and challenges. *AI Perspectives, 1*(1), 1–7.

Helm, J. M., Swiergosz, A. M., Haeberle, H. S., Karnuta, J. M., Schaffer, J. L., Krebs, V. E., et al. (2020). Machine learning and artificial intelligence: Definitions, applications, and future directions. *Current Reviews in Musculoskeletal Medicine, 13*(1), 69–76.

Hinojo-Lucena, F. J., Aznar-Díaz, I., Cáceres-Reche, M. P., & Romero-Rodríguez, J. M. (2019). A tour of open universities through literature: A bibliometric analysis. *The International Review of Research in Open and Distance Learning, 20*(4), 116–131.

Hwang, G. J., & Tu, Y. F. (2021). Roles and research trends of artificial intelligence in mathematics education: A bibliometric mapping analysis and systematic review. *Mathematics, 9*(6), 584.

Hwang, G. J., Xie, H., Wah, B. W., & Gašević, D. (2020). Vision, challenges, roles and research issues of artificial intelligence in education. *Computers and Education: Artificial Intelligence, 1*, 100001.

Imberman, S. (2004). A laboratory exercise using LEGO handy board robots to demonstrate neural networks in an artificial intelligence class. *Accessible hands-on artificial intelligence and robotics education* (pp. 77–81). Association for the Advancement of Artificial Intelligence, https://www.aaai.org/Papers/Symposia/Spring/2004/SS-04-01/SS04-01-016.pdf

ISTE. (2022). *Hands-on AI projects for the classroom a guide for computer science teachers.* Retrieved from https://cdn.iste.org/www-root/Libraries/ Documents%20%26%20Files/Artificial%20Intelligence/AIGDCS_0820-red. pdf?_ga=2.157038398.42578658.1661356230-1998417912.1661356230

Julie, H., Alyson, H., & Anne-Sophie, C. (2020, October). Designing digital literacy activities: An interdisciplinary and collaborative approach. In *2020 IEEE Frontiers in Education Conference (FIE)* (pp. 1–5). IEEE.

Kahn, K. M., & Carlsson, M. (1985). *A grammar kit in Prolog. Uppsala University. Uppsala Programming Methodology and Artificial Intelligence Laboratory.* Retrieved from https://www. softwarepreservation.org/projects/prolog/uppsala/doc/Kahn_Carlsson-UPMAIL-TR-14C.pdf

Kandlhofer, M., Steinbauer, G., Hirschmugl-Gaisch, S., & Huber, P. (2016, October) Artificial intelligence and computer science in education: From kindergarten to university. In *2016 IEEE Frontiers in Education Conference (FIE)* (pp. 1–9). IEEE.

Klassner, F. (2002, February). A case study of LEGO Mindstorms'™ suitability for artificial intelligence and robotics courses at the college level. In *Proceedings of the 33rd SIGCSE Technical Symposium on Computer Science Education* (pp. 8–12).

Liang, T. P., Robert, L., Sarker, S., Cheung, C. M., Matt, C., Trenz, M., & Turel, O. (2021). *Artificial intelligence and robots in individuals' lives: How to align technological possibilities and ethical issues. Internet Research* (Vol. 31, pp. 1–10).

Lichtenthaler, U. (2018). Substitute or synthesis: The interplay between human and artificial intelligence. *Research-Technology Management, 61*(5), 12–14.

Lin, P., & Van Brummelen, J. (2021, May). Engaging teachers to co-design integrated AI curriculum for K-12 classrooms. In *Proceedings of the 2021 CHI Conference on Human Factors in Computing Systems* (pp. 1–12).

Long, D., & Magerko, B. (2020, April). What is AI literacy? Competencies and design considerations. In *Proceedings of the 2020 CHI Conference on Human Factors in Computing Systems* (pp. 1–16).

McCarthy, J. (2007). From here to human-level AI. *Artificial Intelligence, 171*(18), 1174–1182.

McGovern, A., & Fager, J. (2007, March). Creating significant learning experiences in introductory artificial intelligence. In *Proceedings of the 38th SIGCSE Technical Symposium on Computer Science Education* (pp. 39–43).

Mota-Valtierra, G., Rodríguez-Reséndiz, J., & Herrera-Ruiz, G. (2019). Constructivism-based methodology for teaching artificial intelligence topics focused on sustainable development. *Sustainability, 11*(17), 4642.

Narahara, T., & Kobayashi, Y. (2018). Personalizing homemade bots with plug & play AI for STEAM education. In *SIGGRAPH Asia 2018 Technical Briefs* (pp. 1–4).

Newell, A., & Simon, H. (1956). The logic theory machine–A complex information processing system. *IRE Transactions on Information Theory, 2*(3), 61–79.

Ng, D. T. K., & Chu, S. K. W. (2021). Motivating students to learn AI through social networking sites: A case study in Hong Kong. *Online Learning, 25*(1), 195–208.

Ng, D. T. K., Leung, J. K. L., Chu, K. W. S., & Qiao, M. S. (2021). AI literacy: Definition, teaching, evaluation and ethical issues. *Proceedings of the Association for Information Science and Technology, 58*(1), 504–509.

Okonkwo, C. W., & Ade-Ibijola, A. (2021). Chatbots applications in education: A systematic review. *Computers and Education: Artificial Intelligence, 2,* 100033.

Pinkwart, N. (2016). Another 25 years of AIED? Challenges and opportunities for intelligent educational technologies of the future. *International Journal of Artificial Intelligence in Education, 26*(2), 771–783.

Rina, R., Kluzer, S., & Punie, Y. (2022). *DigComp 2.2: The digital competence framework for citizens-with new examples of knowledge, skills and attitudes* (No. JRC128415). Joint Research Centre (Seville site).

Rodríguez-García, J. D., Moreno-León, J., Román-González, M., & Robles, G. (2021, March). Evaluation of an online intervention to teach artificial intelligence with learningml to 10-16-year-old students. In *Proceedings of the 52nd ACM Technical Symposium on Computer Science Education* (pp. 177–183).

Roll, I., & Wylie, R. (2016). Evolution and revolution in artificial intelligence in education. *International Journal of Artificial Intelligence in Education, 26*(2), 582–599.

Sabuncuoglu, A. (2020, June). Designing one year curriculum to teach artificial intelligence for middle school. In *Proceedings of the 2020 ACM Conference on Innovation and Technology in Computer Science Education* (pp. 96–102).

Steinbauer, G., Kandlhofer, M., Chklovski, T., Heintz, F., & Koenig, S. (2021). A differentiated discussion about AI education K-12. *KI-Künstliche Intelligenz, 35*(2), 131–137.

Toivonen, T., Jormanainen, I., Kahila, J., Tedre, M., Valtonen, T., & Vartiainen, H. (2020, July). Co-designing machine learning apps in K–12 with primary school children. In *2020 IEEE 20th International Conference on Advanced Learning Technologies (ICALT)* (pp. 308–310). IEEE.

Touretzky, D., Gardner-McCune, C., Martin, F., & Seehorn, D. (2019, July). Envisioning AI for K-12: What should every child know about AI?. In *Proceedings of the AAAI Conference on Artificial Intelligence* (Vol. 33, No. 01, pp. 9795–9799).

Wallace, S. A., McCartney, R., & Russell, I. (2010). Games and machine learning: A powerful combination in an artificial intelligence course. *Computer Science Education, 20*(1), 17–36.

Wang, P. (2019). On defining artificial intelligence. *Journal of Artificial General Intelligence, 10*(2), 1–37.

Wang, T., & Cheng, E. C. K. (2021). An investigation of barriers to Hong Kong K-12 schools incorporating artificial intelligence in education. *Computers and Education: Artificial Intelligence, 2,* 100031.

Williamson, B., & Eynon, R. (2020). Historical threads, missing links, and future directions in AI in education. *Learning, Media and Technology, 45*(3), 223–235.

Wong, G. K., Ma, X., Dillenbourg, P., & Huan, J. (2020). Broadening artificial intelligence education in K-12: Where to start? *ACM Inroads, 11*(1), 20–29.

Xia, Q., Chiu, T. K., Lee, M., Sanusi, I. T., Dai, Y., & Chai, C. S. (2022). A self-determination theory (SDT) design approach for inclusive and diverse artificial intelligence (AI) education. *Computers & Education, 189,* 104582.

Yau, K. W., Chai, C. S., Chiu, T. K., Meng, H., King, I., & Yam, Y. (2022). A phenomenographic approach on teacher conceptions of teaching artificial intelligence (AI) in K-12 schools. *Education and Information Technologies,* 1–24.

Zawacki-Richter, O., Marín, V. I., Bond, M., & Gouverneur, F. (2019). Systematic review of research on artificial intelligence applications in higher education–where are the educators? *International Journal of Educational Technology in Higher Education, 16*(1), 1–27.

Zhang, K., & Aslan, A. B. (2021). AI technologies for education: Recent research & future directions. *Computers and Education: Artificial Intelligence, 2,* 100025.

Chapter 3
AI Literacy for All

Artificial intelligence (AI) has influenced various industries (e.g., business, science, art, education) rather than merely computer science fields to improve working and learning efficiency. There are many AI-driven applications in daily life (e.g., smart home appliances, smartphones, Google, Siri) to enhance user experience and help people lead a better life. To prepare students to be more ready for tomorrow's workplace, recent studies suggest the importance of learning AI for all students such as how computers learn from its data, the strengths and weaknesses of AI-driven applications, and its ethical concerns about AI (e.g., Long & Magerko, 2020; Ng & Chu, 2021; Sing et al., 2022). Studies suggest that even learners as young as kindergarteners should start to learn AI so that educators can bring them up to become responsible digital citizens (Su & Yang, 2022; Su & Zhong, 2022; Williams et al., 2019a, b). This chapter posits AI literacy should be acquired by all learners, while differences lie in the content and approach at different education levels, i.e., K–16. For example, many countries have started to discuss how to incorporate AI curricula in primary and secondary levels. However, seldom do studies discover why AI should be taught at kindergarten and noncomputer university education. A list of reasons why people should learn AI is discussed in this chapter.

3.1 AI for Living, Workplace, Learning, and Societal Good

Artificial intelligence has made great influences in our everyday lives, not only in technical areas but across industries. Countries/regions have incorporated AI into computer science education, and AI has been added to some of the global digital competency frameworks (e.g., ISTE, DigComEdu) to update the latest educational standards for K–16 learners. There is a great demand to foster students' AI literacy to prepare for valuable abilities and skills before entering the workforce. Learning

© The Author(s), under exclusive license to Springer Nature Switzerland AG 2022
D. T. K. Ng et al., *AI Literacy in K-16 Classrooms*,
https://doi.org/10.1007/978-3-031-18880-0_3

and understanding what AI is, how it works, and its affordances are the first steps to successful study and career in the future. The following sections suggest four major reasons why students should learn AI.

3.1.1 AI for Living

AI is transforming every walk of life and has a great impact on our society. The first reason why all learners need to learn AI is that it enhances people's living standards. First of all, it is a driving force behind social media that AI is used to personalize what is seen on the social media feed through evaluation of post history to identify people's interests and make appropriate suggestions. A University of Oxford's study shows that AI will soon become as advanced as human beings in translating languages by 2024, writing school essays by 2026, selling goods by 2031, writing a bestselling book by 2049, and conducting surgeries by 2053 (Freeman, 2018). Since AI will improve human's lives in almost everything and improve our living standard, there is a need to foster citizens and young learners to become AI literates so that people can use AI-driven tools and interact with others in an appropriate, responsible, and empowered manner (Calzada et al., 2021).

Second, technology companies are exaggerating the capabilities of AI in their products (Surden, 2018). Consumers who understand basic AI algorithms will not be easily tricked by popular media and advertisements. They can think critically about what counts as AI, question the features the AI offers, and think about the ethical concerns and limitations behind. On the other hand, consumers should also be responsible users. Both producers and consumers should handle AI with good intentions to empower human lives. Studies have shown that teaching digital citizenship is essential to help people achieve and understand digital literacy and digital responsibility and ensure safety (Robinson, 2020), digital wealth, and wellness (Jeske et al., 2021). Overall, as one of the most important technological skills, educators can instill learners with AI knowledge and skills to succeed as lifetime learners with AI literacy, so that our future generations could wisely and ethically facilitate their living, working, and learning.

3.1.2 AI for Workplaces

The advancement of AI in turn raises the concern by people that AI will take over millions of current jobs and disrupt the labor force in some occupations (Agarwal, 2018). However, according to the World Economic Forum (2021)'s report, AI is expected to replace 97 millions of jobs worldwide by 2025, and at the same time it will create many job opportunities in many industries. One thing that is certain, AI will soon change the future workplace, but workers and students may not be ready to equip with the related capabilities to fill these new job opportunities. Some speculate that 15% of the working hours will be automated and clerical jobs will be easily eliminated by AI (Manyika et al., 2017). Therefore, it is essential to equip young learners with fundamental AI knowledge, technologies, and mindsets for digital workplace challenges in the future.

Instead of viewing AI as a competitor to work labor, AI can generate compelling benefits for people, industries, and business, thus raising people's working productivity and economic growth. There is a widespread shortage of AI professionals that possess the required skills and knowledge. In recent years, governments, companies, and institutions start to upskill and reskill their employees to harness opportunities of using AI technologies to enhance their working efficiency and be aware of ethical implications and risks (Johnson et al., 2021). For example, Tesla CEO Elon Musk claimed in 2021 that his company was in the advanced stages of developing an autonomous android that would relieve humans of their hazardous, repetitive and boring jobs. The electric-vehicle maker's humanoid Optimus robots could be in production by the end of 2023 and the company plans to deploy thousands of the robots to help resolve future labor shortages for the U.S. economy (Masunaga, 2022). Robots and AI are expected to permeate our daily lives by 2025 (Stahl, 2021). There is a strong need to enforce on-the-job training and vocational and university education to support workers and university students in adapting to AI-enhanced ways of working. With adequate training, young learners could equip themselves with AI competencies to gain a competitive advantage at work, equip with futuristic skills, and fulfill job demands in the AI industry.

3.1.3   AI for Learning

AI-driven technologies have created opportunities for enhancing learning experience through intelligent tutoring, individualized learning, and recommendation systems (Zawacki-Richter et al., 2019). However, students may not be familiar with these novel technologies to facilitate their learning in terms of student cognition, engagement, and collaboration. For example, students could use virtual assistants like Google translation to facilitate their reading and writing (Godwin-Jones, 2011) and interact with chatbots to gain new knowledge (Okonkwo & Ade-Ibijola, 2021). Moreover, PowerPoint includes some AI features (e.g., Design Ideas, Presenter Coach) which enable users to stylish their presentations and make inclusive presentations with live captions and subtitles that gives 88% accuracy while predicting the confidence level of the students. In this way, users can generate stunning presentations, and practice their presentation skills (Microsoft, 2019). However, students may meet challenges such as technological difficulties, communication, and collaboration when using these technologies (e.g., Vincent-Lancrin & van der Vlies, 2020; Zhang et al., 2021). Students who are equipped with AI basic competency would outperform others compared to their counterparts and enjoy the AI-driven learning experiences (Hwang et al., 2022). Therefore, there is a need for educators to develop students' AI literacy so as to adapt to digital transformation in their learning environments.

3.1.4 AI for Societal Good

Countries across the globe face a growing set of shared challenges that will require the next generation to learn, build and connect to identify practical and innovative solutions. AI presents an opportunity to build better tools and solutions that help address some of the world's challenging issues, and deliver positive social impact in accordance with the priorities outlined in the United Nations' 17 Sustainable Development Goals. The AI for Social Good movement aims to establish interdisciplinary partnerships centered around AI applications towards SDGs (Tomašev et al., 2020).

AI could advance human's sustainable development and solve future global challenges about environmental, humanistic issues, accessibility, health, and cultural heritage (Microsoft, 2021). For example, planetary computers were created to build a global environmental network, empower organizations and individuals working to advance sustainability to solve today's environmental challenges (Vinuesa et al., 2020). AI for health empowers researchers and AI institutions to improve the health of people and communities around the world (Reddy et al., 2020). AI can help improve global independence and inclusion in society to make a better living environment, community, education, and employment. Moreover, it supports humanistic response, refugees, displaced persons, human rights, the needs of women and children, preservation and enrichment of cultural heritage (Tomašev et al., 2020). In K-16 education, educators need to equip young learners to become future-ready with the digital and sustainable mindset so that they could help solve these world's challenges when they grow up. To address these global challenges, the idea "AI for societal good" is prominent that everyone should learn AI to solve future global challenges and enhance humans' living standard.

3.2 Benefits of AI Literacy for Different Educational Levels

This section further discussion the specific major reasons why AI should be taught to promote digital citizenship to facilitate people's living, working, and learning to build a better society, the following section further discusses the specific reasons for learners to learn AI at different educational levels: kindergarteners, primary and secondary students, and noncomputer science university students.

3.2.1 Kindergarteners

Nowadays, there are many sophisticated and robotic toys available for children. Children can engage in playful experience and conversations with artificially intelligent assistants such as Siri and Alexa. Scholars proposed that learners as young as 3/4 years old could have the ability to start exploring AI in a simple and foundational manner (Preface, 2021; Su & Yang, 2022; Su et al., 2022). Children are rapid and curious learners. Learning AI can be a very fun and rewarding educational experience if suitable learning methods and tools are used (Preface, 2021). For example, Williams (2018) and Williams et al. (2019a, b) used the suitable learning tool to help children understand the concept of AI through PopBots. Other studies also pointed out that children can experience AI knowledge through different programming toys, such as PopBots, Zhorai, and Teachable Machine (Williams, 2018; Williams et al. 2019a, b; Lin et al., 2020; Vartiainen et al., 2020). Furthermore, some studies found that learning AI can enhance children's cognitive and social development, such as improving their inquiry skills (Kewalramani et al., 2021), foster students' reading literacy about technology (Mah et al., 2021), improve students' adaptive behavior (Shin et al., 2012), and promote interaction and collaboration among children via social robots (Prentzas, 2013). Therefore, it is possible for kindergarten children to develop AI literacy as a complement to their stages of cognitive development.

3.2.2   Primary and Secondary Education

Many view AI literacy as a crucial component of national strategy for digital citizenship education (Seldon & Abidoye, 2018). In today's digital world, learning how to interact with and communicate using AI tools is evident in almost all aspects of everyday life. However, most young students are AI "illiterates" and do not understand the technologies behind (McStay & Rosner, 2021). Recent discussions have also sparked discussions about the importance of learning AI ethics (Borenstein & Howard, 2021; Hagendorff, 2020) and equipping young children with proper mindsets (Floridi et al., 2018).

The goal of implementing AI literacy education at primary and secondary level is not to train and nurture computer programmers. Instead, it aims to offer students hands-on experience and enable them to solve problems, interact with, and communicate with AI tools in everyday life (Ng et al., 2021a, b). It enhances students' AI knowledge and basic digital skills using the latest technologies such as chatbots and intelligent agents. Students need to learn how to evaluate, communicate, and collaborate effectively with AI and use AI as a tool ethically online, at home, and in the future workplace (Long & Magerko, 2020). Aligned with other technological skills like computational thinking, students were not merely the end users of the AI technologies; they needed to learn how to solve problems using AI in authentic settings.

Another trend is that primary and secondary schools have placed high emphasis in STEM education. Young students should learn how to use AI technologies to help solve problems and enhance their working and learning efficiency. For example, students can use automatic translation and grammatical checking tools to facilitate their writing (Lee, 2020). They can use AI tools to adjust parameters (e.g., ages, gender) of people and stylize paintings and photos in their social media feeds (Greenfield, 2021). These examples demonstrated that students with stronger AI literacy skills can outperform their counterparts to live, work, and learn efficiently in the twenty-first century.

We recognize the need for introducing AI into primary and secondary education to foster their digital literacy skills. The authors worked with university professors, local AI developers, and primary and secondary teachers to develop one of the first AI literacy curricula called "AI for All" (Ng et al., 2021). The program has been successfully implemented in a number of primary and secondary schools in Hong Kong. In the academic year of 2021/22, a secondary school helped Clearbot (a local start-up) design an autonomous trash-collecting boat that can identify floating garbage and clean the harbor (HKET, 2022). A primary school worked with local environmentalists to design an AI-empowered scarecrow to fright pests left and grow morecrops.

3.2.3   Noncomputer Science University Students

Industries have started to upskill and reskill their employees in their fields to expose learners to AI. Moreover, graduates who are AI literates can enhance their employability and working efficiency to help them solve authentic problems in workplaces. Therefore, universities have started to engage students from diverse study backgrounds in AI literacy programs to build up their foundational AI knowledge and support them to solve problems by developing AI applications (e.g., Kong et al., 2021). Courses have different focuses for a diverse population of AI literates to tackle skill gaps to expand learning opportunities for all learners. For example, some courses may not focus on mathematical formulae and programming since most students do not need to learn the underlying mathematical and technical concepts behind the AI technologies (Long & Magerko, 2020). Some courses focus on supporting professionals in a particular industry (e.g., healthcare, business, law) how to manipulate the AI-driven systems and machines to enhance their working efficiency, collaborate with their colleagues, and know the ethical concerns and limitations behind the technologies (e.g., Hwang et al., 2022; Xu & Babaian, 2021).

As such, we can see that there is a need to boost students' technical skills and how to apply to AI to meet the career and industrial needs. The goal of these types of courses aims to speak directly to the skills that employers are actively seeking within the AI development sector (e.g., Python programming, machine learning, robotics, data science). These discipline-specific AI courses and programs can expose learners to the most in-demand topics within AI and underpin AI applications and knowledge that are related to their fields. In this way, students are digitally ready to tackle problems of the near future after graduation. Not only will learners enhance their practical application of AI but also attain a credible qualification focused on AI to enhance their employability. Proficiency in AI is highly valued in today's companies. Consequently, this may lead to career prospects in developing, managing, and planning AI solutions for a variety of businesses.

3.3 Conclusion

In this chapter, we presented four major reasons why all citizens should learn AI (for living, workplaces, learning, and society good), and its particular reasons why AI literacy is important at each educational level (kindergarten, primary school, secondary school, and noncomputer science university level). Recent trends from machine learning to algorithms and robotics make AI literacy education prevalent in the education field. Universities and K–12 schools encompass an extensive range of topics such as AI, machine learning tools, and related techniques that are practical to many industries. In these programs, students can learn how AI works and what it is, but, most importantly, how to implement it in real-world scenarios and job roles is paramount to integrating new competence into the changing technological landscape. Students with AI literacy skills can enhance their living standards, use AI applications ethically and wisely, enhance their learning and working effectiveness, be at the forefront of the future, enhance their employability, advance their study after graduation, and be adaptive to the rapidly updating and changing learning tools and environment.

References

Agarwal, P. K. (2018). Public administration challenges in the world of AI and bots. *Public Administration Review, 78*(6), 917–921.

Borenstein, J., & Howard, A. (2021). Emerging challenges in AI and the need for AI ethics education. *AI and Ethics, 1*(1), 61–65.

Calzada, I., Pérez-Batlle, M., & Batlle-Montserrat, J. (2021). People-centered smart cities: An exploratory action research on the cities' coalition for digital rights. *Journal of Urban Affairs, 44*, 1–26.

Floridi, L., Cowls, J., Beltrametti, M., Chatila, R., Chazerand, P., Dignum, V., Luetge, C., Madelin, R., Pagallo, U., Rossi, F., Schafer, B., Valcke, P., & Vayena, E. (2018). AI4People—An ethical framework for a good AI society: Opportunities, risks, principles, and recommendations. *Minds and Machines, 28*(4), 689–707.

Freeman, R. B. (2018). Ownership when AI robots do more of the work and earn more of the income. *Journal of Participation and Employee Ownership, 1*(1), 74–95.

Godwin-Jones, R. (2011). Mobile apps for language learning. *Language Learning & Technology, 15*(2), 2–11.

Greenfield, G. (2021). Artificial life and artificial intelligence advances in the visual arts. *Artificial intelligence and the arts* (pp. 3–26). Springer.

Hagendorff, T. (2020). The ethics of AI ethics: An evaluation of guidelines. *Minds and Machines, 30*(1), 99–120.

HKET. (2022). *Middle school students create AI-powered robotic boats to help clean up marine garbage in Deep Water Bay.* Retrieved from shorturl.at/elsV0

Hwang, G. J., Tu, Y. F., & Tang, K. Y. (2022). AI in online-learning research: Visualizing and interpreting the journal publications from 1997 to 2019. *The International Review of Research in Open and Distance Learning, 23*(1), 104–130.

Jeske, T., Terstegen, S., & Stahn, C. (2021). Opportunities of digitalization and artificial intelligence for occupational safety and health in production industry. *International conference on human-computer interaction* (pp. 43–57). Springer.

Johnson, M., Jain, R., Brennan-Tonetta, P., Swartz, E., Silver, D., Paolini, J., et al. (2021). Impact of big data and artificial intelligence on industry: Developing a workforce roadmap for a data driven economy. *Global Journal of Flexible Systems Management, 22*(3), 197–217.

Kewalramani, S., Kidman, G., & Palaiologou, I. (2021). Using artificial intelligence (AI)- interfaced robotic toys in early childhood settings: A case for children's inquiry literacy. *European Early Childhood Education Research Journal, 29*(5), 652–668.

Kong, S. C., Cheung, W. M. Y., & Zhang, G. (2021). Evaluation of an artificial intelligence literacy course for university students with diverse study backgrounds. *Computers and Education: Artificial Intelligence, 2,* 100026.

Lee, S. M. (2020). The impact of using machine translation on EFL students' writing. *Computer Assisted Language Learning, 33*(3), 157–175.

Lin, P., Van Brummelen, J., Lukin, G., Williams, R., & Breazeal, C. (2020, April). Zhorai: Designing a conversational agent for children to explore machine learning concepts. *Proceedings of the AAAI Conference on Artificial Intelligence, 34*(09), 13381–13388.

Long, D., & Magerko, B. (2020, April). What is AI literacy? Competencies and design considerations. In *Proceedings of the 2020 CHI Conference on Human Factors in Computing Systems* (pp. 1–16).

Mah, G., Hu, X., & Yang, W. (2021). Digital technology use and early reading abilities among bilingual children in Singapore. *Policy Futures in Education, 19*(2), 242–258.

Manyika, J., Chui, M., Miremadi, M., Bughin, J., George, K., Willmott, P., & Dewhurst, M. (2017). A future that works: AI, automation, employment, and productivity. *McKinsey Global Institute Research, Tech. Rep, 60,* 1–135.

Masunaga, S. (2022). *Will Elon Musk's Tesla Bot replace human workers? Don't bet on it.* Retrieved from https://www.latimes.com/business/story/2022-09-30/tesla-automation-workforce.

McStay, A., & Rosner, G. (2021). Emotional artificial intelligence in children's toys and devices: Ethics, governance and practical remedies. *Big Data & Society, 8*(1), 2053951721994877.

Microsoft. (2019) *4 ways AI in PowerPoint will help you nail your next presentation.* Retrieved from   https://news.microsoft.com/en-in/4-ways-ai-in-powerpoint-will-help-you-nail-your-next-presentation/

Microsoft. (2021). *AI for good.* Retrieved from https://www.microsoft.com/en-us/ai/ai-for-good

Ng, T. K., & Chu, S. K. W. (2021). Motivating students to learn AI through social networking sites: A case study in Hong Kong. *Online Learning, 25*(1), 195–208.

Ng, D.T.K., Lai, L.F.W., & Cheung T.W.T. (2021). Artificial Intelligence for All. eFunLearning Ltd., Hong Kong Science and Technology Parks, Hong Kong.

Ng, D. T. K., Leung, J. K. L., Chu, S. K. W., & Qiao, M. S. (2021a). Conceptualizing AI literacy: An exploratory review. *Computers and Education: Artificial Intelligence, 2,* 100041.

Ng, D. T. K., Leung, J. K. L., Chu, K. W. S., & Qiao, M. S. (2021b). AI literacy: Definition, teaching, evaluation and ethical issues. *Proceedings of the Association for Information Science and Technology, 58*(1), 504–509.

Okonkwo, C. W., & Ade-Ibijola, A. (2021). Chatbots applications in education: A systematic review. *Computers and Education: Artificial Intelligence, 2,* 100033.

Preface. (2021). *The ultimate guide for artificial intelligence (AI) for kids.* Retrieved from https://www.preface.ai/blog/kids-learning/ai-for-kids

Prentzas, J. (2013). Artificial intelligence methods in early childhood education. In *Artificial Intelligence, evolutionary computing and metaheuristics* (pp. 169–199). Springer.

Reddy, S., Allan, S., Coghlan, S., & Cooper, P. (2020). A governance model for the application of AI in health care. *Journal of the American Medical Informatics Association, 27*(3), 491–497.

Robinson, S. C. (2020). Trust, transparency, and openness: How inclusion of cultural values shapes Nordic national public policy strategies for artificial intelligence (AI). *Technology in Society, 63,* 101421.

Seldon, A., & Abidoye, O. (2018). *The fourth education revolution.* Legend Press Ltd..

Shin, S., Koh, M. S., & Yeo, M. H. (2012). A comparative study of the preliminary effects in the levels of adaptive behaviors: Learning program for the development of children with autism (LPDCA). *Journal of the International Association of Special Education, 13*(1), 6.

Sing, C. C., Teo, T., Huang, F., & Chiu, T. K. (2022). Secondary school students' intentions to learn AI: Testing moderation effects of readiness, social good and optimism. *Educational Technology Research and Development, 70*(3), 765–782.

Stahl, A. (2021). *The rise of artificial intelligence: Will robots actually replace people?* Retrieved from https://www.forbes.com/sites/ashleystahl/2022/05/03/the-rise-of-artificial-intelligence-will-robots-actually-replace-people/?sh=3cbae7203299.

Su, J., & Yang, W. (2022). *Artificial intelligence in early childhood education: A scoping review* (p. 100049). Artificial Intelligence.

Su, J., & Zhong, Y. (2022). Artificial intelligence (AI) in early childhood education: Curriculum design and future directions. *Computers and Education: Artificial Intelligence, 3*, 100072.

Su, J., Zhong, Y., & Ng, D. T. K. (2022). *A meta-review of literature on educational approaches for teaching AI at the K-12 levels in the Asia-Pacific region* (p. 100065). Artificial Intelligence.

Surden, H. (2018). Artificial intelligence and law: An overview. *Georgia State University Law Review, 35*, 1305.

Tomašev, N., Cornebise, J., Hutter, F., Mohamed, S., Picciariello, A., Connelly, B., ... & Clopath, C. (2020). AI for social good: unlocking the opportunity for positive impact. *Nature Communications, 11*(1), 1–6.

Vartiainen, H., Tedre, M., & Valtonen, T. (2020). Learning machine learning with very young children: Who is teaching whom? *International Journal of Child-Computer Interaction, 25*, 100182.

Vincent-Lancrin, S., & van der Vlies, R. (2020). *Trustworthy artificial intelligence (AI) in education: Promises and challenges.* Retrieved from https://www.oecd-ilibrary.org/content/paper/a6c90fa9-en

Vinuesa, R., Azizpour, H., Leite, I., Balaam, M., Dignum, V., Domisch, S., ... & Fuso Nerini, F. (2020). The role of artificial intelligence in achieving the Sustainable Development Goals. *Nature Communications, 11*(1), 1–10.

Williams, R. (2018). *PopBots: Leveraging social robots to aid preschool children's artificial intelligence education* (Doctoral dissertation, Massachusetts Institute of Technology).

Williams, R., Park, H. W., & Breazeal, C. (2019a, May). A is for artificial intelligence: The impact of artificial intelligence activities on young children's perceptions of robots. In *Proceedings of the 2019 CHI Conference on Human Factors in Computing Systems* (pp. 1–11).

Williams, R., Park, H. W., Oh, L., & Breazeal, C. (2019b, July). Popbots: Designing an artificial intelligence curriculum for early childhood education. *Proceedings of the AAAI Conference on Artificial Intelligence, 33*(01), 9729–9736.

Xu, J. J., & Babaian, T. (2021). Artificial intelligence in business curriculum: The pedagogy and learning outcomes. *The International Journal of Management Education, 19*(3), 100550.

Zawacki-Richter, O., Marín, V. I., Bond, M., & Gouverneur, F. (2019). Systematic review of research on artificial intelligence applications in higher education–where are the educators? *International Journal of Educational Technology in Higher Education, 16*(1), 1–27.

Zhang, D., Mishra, S., Brynjolfsson, E., Etchemendy, J., Ganguli, D., Grosz, B., ... & Perrault, R. (2021). The AI index 2021 annual report. *arXiv preprint arXiv:2103.06312.*

Chapter 4
The Landscape of AI Literacy

This chapter introduced various models of AI literacy education, in particular building on the twenty-first century skills framework to comprise important digital skill sets in today's digital world. Such skills are essential given the challenges brought about by technological advances and changes in the global economic structure to keep the educational standards across regions. This chapter examines how AI is adapted from other digital literacies, the global movement of AI literacy education, and a broad scope of AI literacy from K–16 education.

4.1 AI Literacy as a Twenty-First Century Skill

The definitions of literacy vary. It commonly refers to "the ability to identify, understand, interpret, create, communicate and compute, using printed and written materials associated with varying contexts" (UNESCO, 2018, p. 2) It involves a continuum of learning in enabling people to achieve their goals, to develop their knowledge and potential, and to participate fully in their community and society. In today's digital world, every citizen needs to engage positively, critically, and competently to effectively communicate and collaborate with others through responsible use of technology (Fleaca & Stanciu, 2019). This term has been extended to new literacies such as media, digital, information, computer, and AI literacy (Kong et al., 2021). Artificial intelligence is affecting our everyday life to the extent where it is important for the new generation to develop the necessary literacies of AI so as to understand and use related technologies (Wong et al., 2020; Ng et al., 2022). To combine AI and literacy, AI literacy means having the essential abilities that people need to live, learn, and work in our digital world through AI-driven technologies, and this should be taught at the K–12 levels (Steinbauer et al., 2021). This provides the foundation that we map these literacy skills in Table 4.1 to view the concept of AI literacy as the focal point of the discussion.

© The Author(s), under exclusive license to Springer Nature Switzerland AG 2022
D. T. K. Ng et al., *AI Literacy in K-16 Classrooms*,
https://doi.org/10.1007/978-3-031-18880-0_4

Table 4.1 Digital literacy skills

Types of literacy skills	Definitions
Computer literacy	The knowledge and ability to use a computer and its software to accomplish practical tasks (Talja et al., 2005)
Digital literacy	It is more than just the technical ability to operate digital devices properly; it comprises a variety of cognitive skills that are utilized in performing digital tasks (Van Laar et al., 2017)
Media literacy	The ability to access, understand, and create communications in a variety of contexts. A media-literate person can think critically about what they see, hear, and read in multiple media (Livingstone, 2004)
Information literacy	The ability to know when there is a need for information, to be able to identify, locate, evaluate, and effectively use that information for the issue or problem at hand (Bruce, 1997)
Technological literacy	The ability to responsibly use appropriate technology in various tasks such as communication, problem-solving, information access, management, and creation across disciplines (Gamire & Pearson, 2006)

Adapted from Chu et al. (2021)

As a part of digital literacy, AI literacy education enables students to develop AI-related technological understanding and the digital competence to use, understand, and create AI solutions. In recent years, scholars have proposed adding "AI literacy" to a set of twenty-first century technological competencies that everyone needs to learn to facilitate their learning, working, and living (Long & Magerko, 2020; Ng et al., 2021). Educational frameworks (e.g., the ISTE, DigCompEdu) have included AI to update the latest educational standards to address digital skill levels across the globe (Demeshkant et al., 2020; Riina et al., 2022). Governments have developed AI curricula to align their educational standards with other neighboring countries (Su et al., 2022). Research examined the effectiveness of their AI curriculum from different perspectives including self-determination theory (Xia et al., 2022), digital readiness, social good and optimism (Sing et al., 2022), learning motivation (Lin & Van Brummelen, 2021), behavioral intentions (Chai et al., 2021), and teacher conceptions (Yau et al., 2022). These studies provide evidence that AI education has become a necessary component for young learners to equip themselves for their future studies and career.

4.2   Emerging Frameworks for AI Literacy Education

A range of international curricula and frameworks have emerged these years to foster young learners' AI literacy. According to the UNESCO (2022)'s survey, there are 14 AI curricula which have been developed by 11 countries. In this section, we review a number of these frameworks for AI literacy skills that have been developed in different educational policy environments around the world. We also look at the education reforms in response to the AI literacy skills frameworks put forward by various governments. Policymakers and curriculum developers who decide to incorporate AI literacy into their curricula could learn from other countries/regions. There are a number of frameworks to map AI curriculum for K–12 education to guide K–12 AI literacy education. This section first suggests two renowned frameworks that were widely discussed and cited in the field of AI literacy education: Long and Magerko (2020)'s AI literacy competency framework and Touretzky et al. (2019)'s five big ideas of AI. Then, we summarize some review papers from various places to inform its current development for educators, schools, and policymakers to implement AI literacy education.

4.2.1   Competencies and Design Considerations

Long and Magerko (2020) presented 17 AI literacy competencies (Table 4.2) and 15 design considerations for AI literacy based on a scoping study of existing research to uncover what AI professionals believe all citizens should know and common perceptions and misconceptions among learners. The framework focuses on what educators should involve in their AI curricula and how they design the instruction of AI literacy education.

4.2.2   The Five "Big Ideas" About AI

Since 2018, the AI4K12 Initiative has been developing national guidelines for AI literacy education in K–12. Touretzky et al. (2019) divided the learning concepts into the five "big ideas" of AI to formulate a sound framework on fostering AI literacy. The guidelines define what every student should know about AI with guidelines and activities that help students to build the competencies. The guideline serves as a framework to build educational standards for curriculum developers and educators on AI concepts, essential knowledge, and skills across educational levels. The five big ideas are summarized below: (1) perception (computers perceive the world using sensors), (2) representation and reasoning (agents maintain representation of the world and use them for reasoning), (3) learning (computers can learn from data), (4) natural interaction (intelligent agents require many kinds of knowledge to interact naturally with humans), and (5) societal impact (AI can impact society in both positive and negative ways). Touretzky et al. (2022) further provides an in-depth look at how K-12 students should be introduced to AI knowledge and skills. This review discusses the general format of the guidelines to highlight the appropriateness of the knowledge and skills. This set of guidelines is informed by the need for alignment with CSTA's K-12 Computer Science Standards, Common Core standards and Next Generation Science Standards. Examples were presented to present the learning progression across grade levels and concepts for a specific grade level. Table 4.3 outlined the five big ideas about AI, and the details of the first four areas have already been available for K–12 educators; however, the fifth big idea is still under development.

Table 4.2 AI literacy competencies (Long & Magerko, 2020)

Competency	Descriptions
1. Recognizing AI	Distinguish between technological artifacts that use and do not use AI
2. Understanding intelligence	Critically analyze and discuss features that make an entity "intelligent," including discussing differences between human, animal, and machine intelligence
3. Interdisciplinarity	Recognize that there are many ways to think about and develop "intelligent" machines. Identify a variety of technologies that use AI, including technology spanning cognitive systems, robotics, and ML
4. General vs narrow AI	Distinguish between general and narrow AI
5. AI strengths and weaknesses	Identify problem types that AI excels at and problems that are more challenging for AI. Use this information to determine when it is appropriate to use AI and when to leverage human skills
6. Imagine future AI	Imagine possible future applications of AI, and consider the effects of such applications on the world
7. Representations	Understand what a knowledge representation is and describe some examples of knowledge representations
8. Decision-making	Recognize and describe examples of how computers reason and make decisions
9. ML steps	Understand the steps involved in machine learning and the practices and challenges that each step entails
10. Human role in AI	Recognize that humans play an important role in programming, choosing models, and fine-tuning AI systems
11. Data literacy	Understand basic data literacy concepts
12. Learning from data	Recognize that computers often learn from data (including one's own data)
13. Critically interpreting data	Understand that data needs interpretation. Describe how the training examples provided in an initial dataset can affect the results of an algorithm
14. Action and reaction	Understand how AI systems act in the world that can be directed by higher-level reasoning or it can be reactive
15. Sensors	Understand what sensors are, recognize how computers perceive the world using sensors, and identify sensors on a variety of devices. Identify different sensors to support computer representation and reasoning
16. Ethics	Identify and describe key ethical concerns about AI (e.g., risks, limitations, privacy, bias, misinformation, ethical decision-making, diversity, transparency, accountability)
17. Programmability	Understand that agents are programmable

Table 4.3 Five big ideas about AI (AIK12, 2022)

Big ideas	Key concepts	Descriptions
Perception	Human vs machines Computer sensors Digital encoding Sensing vs perception Feature extraction Abstraction via language and vision Types of domain knowledge	Computers perceive the world using sensors in which perception is the extraction of meaning from sensory information using knowledge Such transformation from signal to meaning takes place in cognitive stages and more abstract features and higher-level knowledge are involved at each stage
Representation and reasoning	Abstraction Symbolic representations Data structures Feature vectors State spaces and operators Combinatorial search Types of reasoning problems Reasoning algorithms	Representations are about data structures that support varying reasoning methods (i.e., algorithms) to operate on real-world problems There are two major types of knowledge representations: symbols and graphs (e.g., queue, stack, map, graph, game board, decision trees, neural network) and numerical representations and feature vectors (i.e., numerical properties of observed phenomena) (e.g., encapsulation, natural language processing, polymorphism) Agents are considered intelligent when they employ a nontrivial sense-deliberate-act cycle to make progress to achieve their goals. In other words, AI needs to sense, deliberate (reason), and act that requires computational sophistication and has significant computing power. For example, electronic door openers are not intelligent agents because their sensing, reasoning, and action are all trivial and simple
Learning	Nature of learning Humans vs machines Finding patterns in data Training a model Using and constructing a reasoning model Adjusting internal representations Learning from experience Neural network Structure of a neural network Weight adjustment Datasets Feature sets Handling large datasets Bias	Machine learning enables a computer to imitate human behaviors without people explicitly programming those behaviors Learning new behaviors results from changes the learning algorithm makes to the internal representations of a reasoning model (e.g., decision tree, neural network) Large training datasets are required to narrow down the learning algorithm's choices when the reasoning model can enable the AI to behave differently The reasoning model constructed by the ML algorithm can be applied to new data to solve problems and make decisions

(continued)

Table 4.3 (continued)

Big ideas	Key concepts	Descriptions
Natural interaction	Nature language (structure of language and applications) Common sense reasoning Understanding emotion Understanding people/philosophy of mind	AI can use natural language to communicate using information, but it is hard to understand human's expression (e.g., metaphor, imagery, humor, emotion) AI can recognize but not experience emotions. Appropriate responses to emotion are necessary to be programmed by humans Current AI systems are narrow reasoners to solve a well-defined problem. It has not yet achieved a very flexible human-like reasoning called broad AI. In other words, the systems lack consciousness and self-awareness. A self-aware computer requires representations of its own existence and thoughts and memories of its past experience
Societal impact	AI ethics, limitations, risks, bias How AI can be applied in positive and negative ways	(The details are still under development by the AIK12)

4.2.3   Other Review Papers in AI Literacy Education

Apart from the two renowned frameworks, other researchers from different countries/regions work rigorously to identify frameworks and timely review AI literacy education.

In *the UK*, Lao (2020) presented a rubric to evaluate ML learning programs and set up the basis for a set of standards in terms of knowledge, skills and attitudes:

- Knowledge: general knowledge, knowledge of methods (e.g., decision trees, neural networks, ensemble methods), bias in ML systems, and societal implications
- Skills: problem scoping, project planning, creating artifacts, analysis of design interactions and results, advocacy, independent out-of-class learning
- Attitudes: interest, identity and community, self-efficacy, persistence

In *Hong Kong*, Su et al. (2022) examined 14 research papers on AI curriculum for K–12 classrooms in the Asia-Pacific region that were taken from 2018 to 2021 by identifying the content knowledge, tools, platforms, activities, theories and models, assessment methods, and learning outcomes of the selected studies.

In *Brazil*, Gresse von Wangenheim et al. (2021) presented a 10-year systematic mapping of emerging visual tools to support the teaching of machine learning in terms of educational characteristics, deployment, and how the tools have been developed and evaluated (e.g., Scratch, App Inventor, mblock, Google Teachable Machine, RapidMiner).

In *Spain*, Rodríguez-García et al. (2020) presented the use of authentic projects to enhance students' higher cognition levels (e.g., creativity, critical thinking) using machine learning models to apply their knowledge and propose solutions to their problems.

And finally in *Finland*, Sanusi et al. (2022) identified the four main categories of resources and tools (conversational agents, programming environment, robotic, and unplugged activity) to document their uses to teach machine learning in K–12 settings from 38 studies. Also from Finland, Tedre et al. (2021) found that students could develop advanced concepts such as machine learning and natural language processing through visualization of concepts using age-appropriate tools. They reviewed 63 documents in the context of computing education to describe the challenges and 13 important characteristics that teachers/students faced in AI literacy courses: (1) new classes of real-world applications for classroom experiments, (2) shift from rule-driven to data-driven thinking, (3) change in the role of syntax and semantics, (4) activities well aligned with modern pedagogy, (5) access to bodily and natural language interaction, (6) a shift away from algorithmic steps, (7) higher level of abstraction and black-boxed mechanisms, (8) a need for new notional machines, (9) new models of testing and debugging, (10) new attributes of goodness of programs, (11) deeper integration with STEAM subjects, (12) ability to explain many services children use daily, and (13) direct connections to topical issues in AI ethics. These studies have been conducted to measure different aspects of AI literacy education in terms of pedagogies, tools, and curriculum. These reviews deal with a number of research focuses: (1) how prepared teachers and schools are in adopting technologies and conducting AI literacy education with a set of design principles, (2) what types of technologies, pedagogies, and content knowledge should be considered to design instruction to foster students' AI literacy, and (3) what are the educational standards that should be met by all students.

4.3   Rising Publications on AI Literacy Education

In the past, teaching AI was not possible in the past for K–12 students and noncomputer science undergraduates. Educators faced challenges in scaffolding K–12 students to understand AI concepts through syntax-based programming (McCarthy, 2007; Wong et al., 2020). In recent years, the emergence of age-appropriate hardwares and softwares enabled educators to improve the learning process for younger learners. The access to a wide range of technologies in day-to-day life, such as chatbots and translation apps, presents opportunities for everyone to understand and use AI in everyday life. This enables educators to leverage on the availability of AI technologies to inculcate AI literacy for young learners. For example, prior studies discussed the potential to incorporate AI learning in K–12 STEAM education via playful experience such as gamified and social media tools to prepare students for future science, technology, engineering, art, and mathematics workforces (e.g., Chiu et al., 2021; Ng & Chu, 2021; Ng et al., 2021).

Knowing and using AI for future careers is only one aspect of teaching AI literacy for educators. Any technology as potent as AI would also bring new risks due to algorithmic bias and malicious uses of AI (Druga et al., 2019; Gong et al., 2020). The importance of the roles of AI ethics is often underemphasized or even overlooked, which is considered as extraneous or surplus to technical concerns in work settings (Hagendorff, 2020). Software developers usually feel a lack of accountability and moral significance of their work, especially when economic incentives are easily overriding commitment to ethical principles and values (Hagendorff, 2020). As such, educating both citizens and computer scientists AI ethics is essential to strengthen their social responsibility and consider social inclusion and diversity to apply AI for societal good (Dignum, 2019).

While the above examples show how substantial AI literacy education can encompass, the arguments are scattered which make scholars difficult to find well-rounded conclusions for development of theoretical frameworks and pragmatic instructional design principles. As such, we find that a systematic search on the works of AI literacy education would be beneficial to elucidating the rising demand. In search of literature on AI literacy, review articles were conducted in two stages. First, we identified 30 peer-reviewed scholarly articles and conference papers from K–12 to higher education levels published from 2016 to 2021 through the Web of Science, Scopus, ProQuest Education Collection, IEEE, and ACM digital library (Ng et al., 2021). A year later in August, the second stage further focused on each school level and selected articles using the same databases to understand how to incorporate AI literacy education across levels.

In Ng et al. (2021)'s review, the Google Scholar search identifies a dramatic increase in AI literacy publications from 2016 to 2022 (see Fig. 4.1). As AI becomes more and more important in work settings and everyday life, researchers began to define AI literacy based on the term "literacy" which has been applied to define skill sets in varied disciplines (Long & Magerko, 2020). Based on 30 selected studies, the countries/regions that published 2 or more AI literacy articles include the United States, China, Hong Kong, Spain, and Austria. Researchers conducted studies and implemented AI literacy interventions across various educational levels. Most of the articles focused on primary school and secondary school students that covered almost half of the reviewed studies. Among these, 14 of the studies are from secondary school level. About one-third of the studies were conducted in an informal setting, which included after-school programs, out-of-school activities, and poster presentations. Seven studies were conducted in regular lessons in a formal setting.

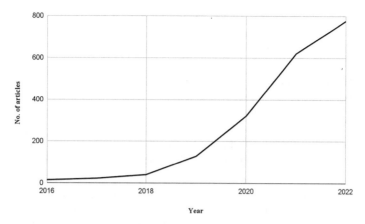

Fig. 4.1 AI literacy articles from Google Scholar published by year (2016–2022)

One possible reason is that AI literacy is an emerging field, and most researchers tend to conduct preliminary studies to explore their interventions in an informal setting or merely write opinion papers based on their observation. Regarding the research method, the empirical studies adopted qualitative methods (12), quantitative methods, (5) and mixed-method approach (8) to evaluate students' AI literacy development.

4.3.1   AI Literacy Education for K–12 Students

The UNESCO report listed 11 countries that have developed government-endorsed AI curricula in K–12 level. The motivations for the development are aimed to improve graduates' capacity, to meet the skills demanded by both the job market and everyday interactions (UNESCO, 2022). They analyzed the curricula and summarized them into nine topic areas of AI K–12 curriculum content and further grouped them into three main categories: (1) AI foundations, (2) ethics and social impact, and (3) understanding, using, and developing AI. As illustrated in the report, AI literacy comprises both data literacy and algorithm literacy, and it serves as an orientation of "knowledge, understanding, skills, and value of AI" (UNESCO, 2022, p. 11).

Other than the examples captured in the UNESCO report, educators have also reported cross-sector projects on the development of AI curriculum. In Hong Kong, Chiu et al. (2021) collaborated with the local government, secondary schools, and industrial partners to create an AI curriculum at the secondary level named AI for the Future (AI4Future). They proposed a curriculum framework that maps their teaching units into five modules: (1) awareness, (2) knowledge, (3) interaction, (4) empowerment, and (5) ethics (AKIEE) (Chiu et al., 2021). Xia et al. (2022) further added inclusion and diversity of education into this AI initiative using self-determination theory to explain student engagement from the needs satisfaction perspective. Likewise, Ng et al. (2021) proposed an AI curriculum called AI for All in primary and secondary schools in Hong Kong to foster students' AI literacy. Pilot studies have been conducted to show the effectiveness of incorporating the curriculum in informal settings through social networking sites (Ng & Chu, 2021), and digital storytelling approach (Ng et al., 2022).

In Europe, Kandlhofer et al. (2016, p. 2) defined AI literacy as the understanding of "the techniques and concepts behind AI products and services instead of just learning how to use certain technologies or current applications". They proposed seven teaching topics to supplement this definition, including: automata, intelligent agents, graphs and data structures, sorting, problem solving by search, classic planning, and machine learning. In the US, MIT's AI experts, researchers, curriculum developers and educators work to set the standard for how middle schoolers learn about AI. They proposed an AI initiative called Responsible AI for Social Empowerment and Education (RAISE) to establish a project-centered curriculum. In the learning programs, students will produce authentic learning artifacts through design thinking projects that are driven by exploring and doing. Along the way students will deepen their understanding of AI literacy, computational action, and ethical thinking (MIT, 2021).

These curricula and frameworks are evidence to show that AI education has moved from a subject specialized by computer science students to a direction where it reaches all education levels and that it is diversified. However, it is noteworthy that the above examples focus on K–12 level while little has been mentioned for postsecondary-level students who have few chances to learn about AI.

4.3.2   AI Literacy Education for Noncomputer Science University Students

To realize the motivations for the growing attention in AI education for noncomputer science undergraduates, Ashok Goel posited three converging factors that would shape AI education to fit for twenty-first century workplaces – (1) the demand created by increasing integration of AI technologies in industries, (2) the rapid diversification of AI education that used to be offered in graduate studies and now spread widely across disciplines and educational levels, and (3) the need for all citizens to be literate in AI such that they aware of the use of AI technologies in their daily lives and be informed of the principles and values behind (Goel, 2017).

The evolution of AI in the past two decades unfolds a broad spectrum of technological applications that affect our daily lives, in particular the rapid development of artificial neural networks (ANN) and deep learning (DL) (Chan & Zary, 2019). Implications are profound, from improving product efficiency, using big data for business strategies and analyses, to individualizing user experiences, etc. For instance, personal mobile devices are a typical example of applying AI features like face recognition for unlocking screens and online payments. The game industry creates AI characters, or non-player characters (NPCs), to make virtual reality experiences more realistic. Educators use generative adversarial networks (GAN) to create new images, videos, or styles for drawing learning. The list goes on. The demand of AI is no longer a privilege to advanced tech companies but an indispensable part of existing and uprising industries. Corporates are looking for future-ready employees who possess high command in tech and AI literacies (Microsoft News Center India, 2022). UNESCO released a report on the global status of AI curricula and described "AI as the basic grammar of our century" (UNESCO, 2022, para. 5). Hence, the need to push forward AI education is not only important for the growth of society but also a matter of urgency.

The report concluded that "all citizens need to be equipped with some level of AI literacy covering the values, knowledge and skills relating to AI" (UNESCO, 2022, p. 61). This notion is agreed by other scholars (e.g., Kong et al., 2021; Long & Magerko, 2020), but they also noted that limited efforts have been made to promote AI literacy for citizens. To generate a structure to classify the data that may emerge from this review and for it to be meaningful, we may address this by looking through the lens of AI literacy. Recent studies have conceptualized the term "AI literacy" by defining what it means, what it comprises, and how it should be assessed; however, there is no universal consensus to a single definition to date. Therefore, Sect. 4.4 summarizes education policies of AI literacy education across the countries/regions, and Sect. 4.5 further categorizes the existing evidence and proposes frameworks on AI literacy, based on three existing consensus educational models.

4.4 New Education Policies on AI Literacy Across the Globe

Learning from the existing frameworks and rising demands of AI literacy mentioned by scholars and practitioners, we see a paradigm shift on the significance of this matter. Not only AI literacy education should be advocated at school and institutional level but also influenced by government or even global policies. This section captures the AI literacy education policy in countries with more than two AI literacy publications in secondary level (i.e., the United States, China, Hong Kong, Spain) and neighboring countries (e.g., Japan, Singapore, Korea) in Ng et al. (2021)'s reviews.

Both the United States and China have made great progress in incorporating AI education into their workforce development and K–12 education systems. However, they are approaching education goals in different ways. The United States is developing AI curricula through industry and university collaboration, whereas China is using its centralized authority to mandate AI curricula in its K–12 education with the support from AI companies that partnered with schools and universities to train students (CSET, 2021). The United States had long led in tech innovation despite strong global competition. Many tech companies (e.g., Microsoft, Apple, Amazon) and organizations (e.g., AIK12) help promote AI literacy education which makes 28 states in the country adopt policies to support K–12 computer science education in 2021. In China, the Education Ministry has introduced AI into the K–12 school curriculum with the first AI textbook supported by SenseTime to learn the basics of image recognition, sound recognition, text recognition, and deep learning across 40 pilot schools in 2018.

In Europe, Spain is also a country with rich research publications in AI literacy education. In 2019, the European Commission has developed the scope of an Erasmus+ project called AI+, which aims to develop an AI curriculum for high school students. The project also supported some neighboring European countries (e.g., Italy, Slovenia, Lithuania, Finland). A year later, another scheme called LearningML was presented to bring the fundamentals of AI to students and people who are interested in acquiring related knowledge. Both initiatives are driven from universities that encourage learners to learn AI literacy at a younger age.

Although other Asian countries did not have many AI literacy publications, their practices and implementation are worthy for policymakers to think behind for referencing.

- Japan: In 2020, a national curriculum mandated CS education is designed to prepare the K–12 students capable of understanding and using AI technologies in their future to maintain the competitiveness of Japan as one of the leading countries in the AI-driven world.
- Singapore: In 2018, the government announced the "AI Singapore" project to develop students' AI capabilities. The project had brought together the research institutions including AI startups and companies to develop AI learning products to grow K–12 students' AI knowledge and develop talents to power Singapore's AI efforts. At the same time, two AI research programs, "AI for Students" and "AI for Kids" had also started.
- Korea: In 2019, the Korean government announced the "National AI Strategy" to enhance the country's AI competitiveness by 2030. The government had made plans to introduce AI to all high school students in 2021 and further extended AI education to kindergartens and primary and middle students by 2025.
- Taiwan: The Ministry of Education (MOE) is promoting AI learning to reshape the school environment to make AI an integral part of students' lives. In 2019, the MOE announced the compulsory integration of AI-related educational materials in public school curriculums from elementary to high school.

Hong Kong has also incorporated AI curricula in K–12 education for a few years. In 2020, an AI curriculum called "AI for Future" was implemented into pre-university education to cultivate the competitiveness of the young generation among 18 schools. A year later, the Hong Kong Education City announced the "Go AI Scheme" which aims to promote AI Education in Hong Kong through introducing self-paced learning platforms and enhancing teachers' and students' AI knowledge and future-ready skills in the twenty-first century. Local researchers (e.g., Chai et al., 2021; Chiu et al., 2021; Ng et al., 2021; Wang & Cheng, 2021) have worked vigorously to promote AI literacy education across educational levels from different perspectives.

4.5 Our Three Proposals of AI Literacy Educational Frameworks (Bloom's, TPACK, P21)

This section builds on a previously developed ideas based on our three recent published systematic reviews (i.e., Ng et al., 2021) reflecting on three classic educational theories (i.e., Bloom's taxonomy, twenty-first century literacy skills, Technological, Pedagogical and Content Knowledge framework). We hope to extend the existing theories to underlie the theoretical contributions and significant advances in AI literacy education studies. First, we applied the Bloom's taxonomy to conceptualize varied cognitive levels across the spectra of AI learning inquiry with four perspectives, namely, know and understand, use and apply, create and evaluate, as well as ethical issues. Then, the Technological, Pedagogical and Content Knowledge (TPACK) framework was also explored in terms of learning artifacts, pedagogical approaches, and subject matters to offer effective means to integrate AI literacy into school curricula and how educators help students develop AI literacy understanding. Lastly, we discuss the need to add AI to twenty-first century literacy in work settings and everyday life and as a fundamental skill for everyone, not just for computer scientists.

4.5.1 AI Literacy and Bloom's Taxonomy

A definition for AI literacy learning is presented in four cognitive domains. Ng et al. (2021) proposed a set of the abilities and skills that has potential to be mapped to the cognitive domains in Bloom's taxonomy, an approach to categorize the levels of reasoning skills and ordered thinking required across different learning contexts. There are six levels in the taxonomy, each requiring a higher level of complexity and ordered thinking from the students. The levels are understood to be successive, so that one level must be mastered before the next level can be reached (Huitt, 2011). The reason why we adopted the Bloom architecture is that AI literacy is novice to educators and a classification of levels of cognitive processes has not yet been developed in the context of AI learning. However, this model is a classic pedagogical theory that establishes the core foundation of AI taught to young learners. In this review, it is proposed to assign these three aspects (i.e., know and understand, use, and evaluate and create AI) into the cognitive levels of Bloom's taxonomy. "Know and understand AI" is assigned to the bottom two levels, "use AI" in applying concepts and applications is assigned to the apply level, and "evaluate and create AI" are assigned to the top three levels to analyze, evaluate, and create AI (see Fig. 4.2).

The AI literacy studies discussed how to foster learners' AI literacy in knowing and understanding AI, as well as how to use AI applications in everyday life and apply its underlying concepts in different contexts. However, according to Ng et al. (2021)'s review, not many studies mentioned how to enhance students to analyze, evaluate, and create AI applications through higher-order thinking activities. A

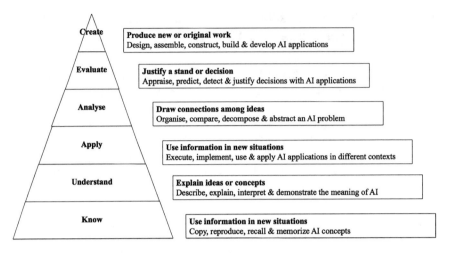

Fig. 4.2 AI literacy and Bloom's taxonomy

Table 4.4 Framework of AI literacy (Ng et al., 2021)

AI literacy	Definitions	Sample studies
Know and understand AI	Know the basic functions of AI and how to use AI applications	Kandlhofer et al. (2016); Robinson et al. (2020)
Use AI	Applying AI knowledge, concepts, and applications in different scenarios	Druga et al. (2019); Julie et al. (2020); Vazhayil et al. (2019)
Evaluate and create AI	Higher-order thinking skills (e.g., evaluate, appraise, predict, design) with AI applications	Druga et al. (2019); How and Hung (2019)
AI ethics	Human-centered considerations (e.g., fairness, accountability, transparency, ethics, safety)	Chai et al. (2020); Druga et al. (2019)

possible reason that existing AI literacy studies focused more on general skills and knowledge about AI is that AI literacy is a set of fundamental skills and abilities in helping everyone, including students and citizens, to acquire, construct, and apply knowledge. They may not necessarily handle how to abstract and decompose AI problems nor build AI applications in everyday lives; instead, they need to know the basic concepts and use AI ethically. As such, it is noticed that prior AI literacy studies put more emphasis on engaging learners in lower-level thinking activities. However, when students are promoted to secondary schools and universities, they become knowledgeable to apply their prior knowledge to create their own artifacts and justify decisions with AI applications and algorithms for their future career. In summary, four aspects of fostering AI literacy were identified from the review (see Table 4.4).

Know and Understand AI Prior studies conceptualize AI literacy as educating learners about acquiring fundamental concepts, skills, knowledge, and attitudes that require no prior knowledge. On top of being the end users of AI applications, learners should understand the technologies behind. Burgsteiner et al. (2016) and Kandlhofer et al. (2016) defined AI literacy as the ability to understand the basic techniques and concepts behind AI in different products and services. Moreover, some researchers associate AI literacy with perceived abilities, confidence, and readiness in learning AI. In K–12 education, Druga et al. (2019) and Lee et al. (2021) designed learning curriculums and activities that foster AI literacy that focuses on how learners gain AI concepts.

Use and Apply AI   Prior research emphasized the importance of educating learners to know how to apply AI concepts in different contexts and applications in everyday life. For example, Rodríguez-García et al. (2020) evaluated LearningML, a machine learning model builder, to educate citizens to understand AI applications and how it can affect our lives, as well as knowing the ethical issues regarding AI technologies. In addition, it is identified that half of the studies in Ng et al. (2021)'s review discussed the human-centered and ethical considerations and focused on using AI concepts and application ethically. Eight out of 30 articles borrowed the ideas of computational thinking to interplay AI literacy and AI thinking (Ng et al., 2021) (see Table 4.5). AI thinking refers to the construction of logic and algorithms in order to support students' understanding of how to use knowledge bases for problem-solving, processing semantics and handling unstructured data (Vazhayil et al., 2019). For example, How and Hung (2019) leveraged AI thinking through conducting data analytics with computing and interpreted new findings from the machine-learned discovery of hidden patterns in data.

Evaluate and Create AI   AI augments human intelligence with digital automation and articles alluded to AI literacy to engage learners in higher-order thinking activities. Two-thirds of AI literacy studies in Ng et al. (2021)'s review had extended AI literacy to higher-order thinking abilities that enabled individuals to critically evalu-

Table 4.5 AI thinking elements

Elements	Descriptions	Examples
AI concepts	Technical and conceptual understanding of the basic AI concepts	Understand the basic AI concepts and their origins such as machine learning, deep learning and neural network
AI practices	The techniques and strategies used when applying AI	Appreciate the real-world applications of AI concepts such as speech recognition, robotics Training, validation, and testing Remixing or reusing code
AI perspectives	Attitudes and dispositions adopted while solving problems	Collaborating to solve problems, understanding of technology as a problem-solving tool Consider the ethical and safety concerns when applying AI technologies in real-world applications

ate AI technologies, communicate, and collaborate effectively with AI (e.g., Long & Magerko, 2020). For example, Han et al. (2019) enhanced students' scientific and technological knowledge which then was applied in scientific research-based learning to solve practical problems. Long and Magerko (2020) engaged citizens in co-creating AI amenities in public spaces to broaden their public AI literacy and experiences. Participants could engage with public interactive artworks' progress sequentially from being initially attracted to an AI-enabled installation to relate their interaction with the installation and other people.

Overall, although there are slight variations on the definition of AI literacy, prior studies support the notion that everyone, especially K–12 students, should acquire basic AI knowledge and abilities, enhance motivation for future career, as well as use AI-enabled technology ethically (Chai et al., 2021). In terms of cognitive domain, AI literacy serves as a set of competencies that enables individuals to know and use AI ethically, critically evaluate AI technologies, communicate, and collaborate effectively with AI (Long & Magerko, 2020).

4.5.2 AI Literacy and TPACK Framework

Inspired from the Technological, Pedagogical and Content Knowledge (TPACK) framework, this section evaluates how educators help learners develop AI literacy skills in terms of pedagogy, content, and pedagogy (see Fig. 4.3). This model enriches the effective means to integrate AI literacy into school curricula and how educators help learners develop AI literacy. The reason that we adopt the TPACK model is that it is widely used across studies to identify how teachers can incorporate technologies into their pedagogical methods and content knowledge and conceptualizes their capacity and knowledge that is needed to integrate relevant technologies in AI literacy education (Koehler et al., 2013). It provides a map for understanding how to integrate AI literacy into classrooms effectively (e.g., Celik, 2022; Kim et al., 2021). For example, Kim et al. (2021) based on AI learning resources to conceptualize TPACK to improve teaching for K–12 AI education, which offers core foundations of AI taught to young learners. Among the three knowledge, technological knowledge involves the affordances and use of domain-specific learning tools such as hardware and software in AI literacy education, AI-enabled tools (e.g., intelligent agents), and unplugged learning tools (e.g., role-playing). Second, pedagogical knowledge relates to teaching methods and their application to promote student AI literacy learning, which entails teaching strategies and scaffolding, feedbacking students' learning processes (Janssen et al., 2019). Third, content knowledge concerns knowledge about the AI literacy subject matter that specific subjects should be covered in the curriculum.

Technological Knowledge Given the complexity of AI, age-appropriate learning artifacts were important to scaffold students' AI conceptual understandings and stimulate their motivation and interest in learning AI. Table 4.6 provides an over-

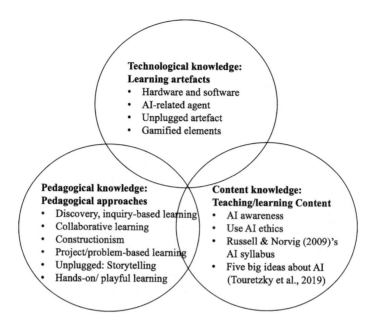

Technological knowledge:
Learning artefacts
- Hardware and software
- AI-related agent
- Unplugged artefact
- Gamified elements

Pedagogical knowledge:
Pedagogical approaches
- Discovery, inquiry-based learning
- Collaborative learning
- Constructionism
- Project/problem-based learning
- Unplugged: Storytelling
- Hands-on/ playful learning

Content knowledge:
Teaching/learning Content
- AI awareness
- Use AI ethics
- Russell & Norvig (2009)'s AI syllabus
- Five big ideas about AI (Touretzky et al., 2019)

Fig. 4.3 AI literacy TPACK framework

view of the types of AI learning artifacts ranging from hardware to software-focused artifacts, intelligent agents, and unplugged learning tools. In recent years, there has been an increase in hardware and software that enhance AI concepts accessible to younger learners. Hardware- and software-focused artifacts engaged students to use physical and digital artifacts to make and create AI-driven applications. For example, Chiu et al. (2021) designed a robotic car called CUHKiCar with built-in AI functions to offer interactive learning experiences for students to do face-tracking and line following tasks. It is found that students obtained a significant improvement in perceived knowledge gain, confidence, motivation, and AI readiness. Another study conducted by Chai et al. (2021) who used a platform in which students could use Alpha dog robots and design algorithms to do recognitions of physical characteristics such as temperature, voice, face, and images. It enables students to use AI and mathematics knowledge (e.g., calculus, statistics) to build their AI solutions.

The popularity of current AI technologies encourages students to make intelligent agents and machine learning models without needing to program such as ML-for-kids and Teachable Machine (Long & Magerko, 2020). In this context, there is an opportunity for educators to provide students access to AI literacy and reinforce the AI concepts through these emerging tools. In addition, AI-driven tools such as chatbot, writing assistants, and web mapping encourage students to experience the technological affordances of AI applications across subject disciplines. This enables students to express knowledge using AI and access the more advanced concepts which was not possible in the past. Alternatively, unplugged learning

Table 4.6 Learning artifacts

	Definition	Learning artifacts examples	Sample studies
Hardware-focused artifacts	Use physical artifacts to learn AI such as robotics, sensors and Arduino devices	Bee-bots, LEGO Mindstorms NXT, Cubelets, alpha dog robot, Kinect LuminAI, VR Robot Improv Circus, Sound Happening, Shape of Story AI home assistants: Jibo robot, Anki's Cozmo robot, and Amazon's Alexa Lego Mindstorms NXT	Kandlhofer et al. (2016); Chai et al. (2021); Long and Magerko (2020); Druga et al. (2019); Burgsteiner et al. (2016)
Software-focused artifacts	Use digital artifacts to learn AI such as block-/ syntax-based programming and simulation	Google maps, Golog, YAGI, ASRAEL SmileyCluster, A* algorithm in C#	Kandlhofer et al. (2016); Wan et al. (2020); Burgsteiner et al. (2016)
AI-related agents	Use intelligent agents such as expert systems, machine learning trainers, and chatbots to build their custom machine learning models without coding	Scratch, Google's Teachable Machine, Generative Adversarial Networks (GANS), Watson AI services, BayesiaLab, AI home assistants: Jibo robot, Anki's Cozmo robot, and Amazon's Alexa	Lee et al. (2021); Vazhayil et al. (2019); How and Hung (2019); Druga et al. (2019)
Unplugged	Use learning activities to learn AI without a computer such as lecture, case study, role-playing, and storytelling	Lectures, career talk, textbook, case study, webinar, role-playing, storytelling	Lee et al. (2021); Rodríguez-García et al. (2020); Julie et al. (2020)

activities were designed to foster students' AI literacy without using a computer through engaging approaches such as case study, role-playing, and storytelling (e.g., Julie et al., 2020; Rodríguez-García et al., 2020).

Pedagogical Knowledge   The pedagogies including teaching methods and strategies are classified according to the levels of education. One of the aims of AI literacy education for secondary schools is to familiarize students with the fundamental concepts of AI/computer science and encourage them to discover the connection between AI applications and the underlying concepts. For example, researchers introduced students to AI concepts in playful and inquiry approaches through robotics making (Kandlhofer et al., 2016), performing Turing test with intelligent agents, creating chatbot and inference algorithms (Wong et al., 2020), and building applications through blockly-based programming (Gong et al., 2020). In addition to understanding the connection between those AI techniques and common AI applications, secondary students should have the abilities to apply prior AI knowledge in practical group projects to analyze and solve problems independently (Kandlhofer et al., 2016). Thus, educators could design real-world, collaborative projects based on the principles of constructionism and instructionism (Kandlhofer et al., 2016).

Researchers suggest various hands-on activities such as robot constructions (Williams et al., 2019), data and comparative visualization (Wan et al., 2020), as well as training AI models (Vazhayil et al., 2019) as possible means to promote AI literacy in secondary school levels.

This section identifies the major three pedagogical methods and strategies that are used in this dissertation: project-/problem-based learning, collaborative learning, and experiential learning via playful games and simulations (see Table 4.7). First, project-/problem-based learning is the learning approach that engages students to gain knowledge and skills by working to investigate authentic questions, problems, or challenges (Kokotsaki et al., 2016). For example, Vachovsky et al. (2016) engaged 24 girls in projects to learn computer visions, robotics, and natural language processing in a summer camp. In the survey, 95.8% of students believed that the projects that students built can help the society. Moreover, students believed that the course was interesting (83.3%) and enhanced their confidence in using AI (75%). Rodríguez-García et al. (2020) presented the LearningML projects (a low floor high ceiling platform to learn machine learning through doing) to bring the fundamentals of machine learning (ML) to students to acquire its knowledge and educate them to become critical thinking citizens. Project-/problem-based learning could provide authentic settings such as building modals of athletic moves (Zimmermann-Niefield et al., 2019), meaningful scientific and STEM contexts that could motivate them to learn AI through a sense of authenticity and real-world applicability (Wan et al., 2020).

Collaborative learning allows students to learn how to communicate and work with classmates to gain AI knowledge and manipulate with smart devices (Roll & Wylie, 2016). For example, Gong et al. (2020) engaged students to take different roles such as project managers, software designers, hardware designers, and art designers to build smart vehicles in authentic settings. Another study conducted by also asked students to be buyers and sellers to find out problems and shortcomings about the intelligent functions in the smart home systems. Kaspersen et al. (2021a) asked students to formulate three to four students of a group to design ML models to predict whether a person will vote for a particular political party. A combination

Table 4.7 Pedagogies of AI literacy education

Pedagogies	Descriptions	Sample studies
Project-/problem-based learning	Learning approaches to engage students to gain knowledge and skills by working to investigate authentic questions, problems, or challenges	Rodríguez-García et al. (2020); Sakulkueakulsuk et al. (2018)
Collaborative learning	This pedagogy allows students to learn how to communicate and work with classmates to gain AI knowledge and manipulate with smart devices	Deng et al. (2021); Gong et al. (2020)
Experiential learning	Process of learning by doing through hands-on experiences and reflection; students could gain better understanding to connect theories and knowledge learned in the classroom to real-world situations	Chiu et al. (2021); Morris (2020); Tamborg et al. (2022)

of collaborative learning and project-/problem-based learning could effectively enhance students' high-order thinking skills such as problem-solving, leadership skills, project management, and creativity (e.g., Deng et al., 2021; Gong et al., 2020). The third common method is to engage students in experiential learning. Experiential learning is the process of learning by doing through hands-on experiences and reflection; students could gain better understanding to connect theories and knowledge learned in the classroom to real-world situations (Morris, 2020). This allows students to explore what ML is via Teachable Machine (Chiu et al., 2021; Tamborg et al., 2022), Code.org games (Ng & Chu, 2021), intelligent agents, chatbot, syntax-based programs (e.g., Python) (Gong et al., 2020; Gunasilan, 2021), and Blockly-based programs (e.g., Scratch, Snap!) (Estevez et al., 2019; Kahn et al., 2018). These activities provide students hands-on experience to explore what AI is, visualize advanced concepts, and build ML models (Reyes et al., 2020). Although these activities offer hands-on experience to scaffold their AI understandings, most studies further applied minds-on collaborative projects to encourage students to further build knowledge through making digital and tangible artifacts in constructionist approaches. In this way, educators could enable students to reach higher cognition levels and apply AI skills and knowledge to solve real-world problems for future learning and career challenges (Chai et al., 2021).

Content Knowledge   In recent years, governments and universities have worked vigorously to design meaningful K–12 learning curricula and activities that focus on different AI concepts and how they apply AI to contexts of their interests (Druga et al., 2019; Lee et al., 2021; UNESCO, 2022). For example, Long and Magerko (2020) proposed 16 competencies that students should learn: recognizing AI, understanding AI, interdisciplinary skills, distinguishing general and narrow AI, identifying strengths and weaknesses of AI, imagining future applications of AI and their societal impacts, knowledge representations, decision-making, understanding machine learning, recognizing the roles of human in AI, data literacy, learning from data, critically interpreting data, higher-level reasoning of AI, sensors, and ethical concerns behind. Touretzky et al. (2019)'s five "big ideas" of AI have set a sound framework for future research on fostering AI literacy:

- Perceptions: Computers perceive the world using sensors.
- Representation and reasoning: Agents maintain representation of the world and use them for reasoning.
- Learning: Computers can learn from large amounts of data.
- Natural interaction: Intelligent agents require many kinds of knowledge to interact naturally with humans.
- Societal impact: AI can impact society in both positive and negative ways.

Wong et al. (2020) categorized AI literacy in K–12 into three dimensions: AI concepts, applications, and ethics. In another study, Chiu et al. (2021) further proposed five modules of AI learning: (1) awareness, (2) knowledge, (3) interaction, (4) empowerment, and (5) ethics. These modules can be categorized into the beginner, intermediate, advanced levels, and caters for capacity building by offering a clear path to the development of student AI techniques and skills. UNESCO (2022) analyzed the government-endorsed curricula in 11 member states and pointed out 3 major categories that AI curricula should have: (1) AI foundations including algorithms and programming, data literacy, and contextual problem-solving; (2) AI ethics, societal implications, and the applications of AI to other domains; and (3) understanding and using AI techniques, understanding and using AI technologies, and developing AI.

However, very few prior studies do not categorize the topic areas according to grade levels. UNESCO (2022) tried to map the learning outcomes of AI curricula from the member states for each education level. It is important for educators to understand the cognitive development of each developmental stage, and we proposed the use of Bloom's taxonomy to categorize the learning contents. To understand what should be taught at the secondary level, prior studies documented that junior secondary students should focus on preliminary and simple AI concepts such as machine learning, natural language processing, and Turing tests (AIK12, 2022; Chiu et al., 2021). Educators should design experiential learning activities for students to have a hands-on experience to taste and use the related AI applications and discuss their benefits, challenges, ethical concerns, and shortcomings of these tools (Sabuncuoglu, 2020). In this way, students needed to apply these knowledge and skills to solve problems using well-defined hardware, software, and intelligent agents. Table 4.8 illustrates the learning contents that were taught in junior and secondary school levels.

4.5.3   AI Literacy and P21's Framework for the 21st Century Learning

Most of the studies focused on students' technological knowledge and skills; however, few of them identify that AI literacy should extend to broader digital competencies that support students to use AI technologies to facilitate their learning. This section highlights the notion that AI literacy should be viewed as an important twenty-first century skill set (Ng et al., 2021). Twenty-first century skills and AI digital competencies are both concepts that focus on a broad spectrum of knowledge, skills, and attitudes that were viewed as essential components of digital literacy in our digital world. Such digital aspects should go beyond technical use and focus more on a more holistic understanding that recognizes other contextual, critical, and complex literacy. In other words, although the term "digital literacy" consists of "digital"; the digital aspect is often seen as a discrete skill, implying that the twenty-first-century skills are not necessarily underpinned by ICT. The focus should be more on knowledge- or content-related skills, instead of technical skills required for the workforce, such as life and career skills, multidisciplinary skills, and learning and innovation skills (National Research Council, 2012; Van Laar et al., 2017).

Table 4.8 Learning contents in primary, junior, and senior secondary school levels

Levels	Learning contents samples	Sample studies
Primary school	*Experiencing AI*: Interacting with AI machines such as driving an AI toy car *AI foundations*: Knowing and understanding basic concepts, vocabulary, history of AI, facial recognition and machine learning, hands-on experience, using applications (e.g., Google's Teachable Machine), and programming tools to solve problems *Societal impacts and AI ethics*: AI ethics, societal impacts of AI, algorithmic bias	Heinze et al. (2010); Narahara & Kobayashi (2018)
Junior secondary	*Experiencing AI*: Using AI applications, benefits, and disadvantages of using AI, machine learning, face recognition, image stylizer, machine generation of creative content, experimentation of using AI technologies *AI foundations*: History/introduction/recent development of AI and its subareas, differences between humans and machines, natural language processing, scratch activities on machine learning and image recognition, machine learning *Societal impacts and AI ethics*: AI ethics, societal impacts of AI, machine reasoning and its bias	Chiu et al. (2021); Fernández-Martínez et al. (2021); Ng and Chu (2021)
Senior secondary	*Complex AI topics*: Natural language processing, computer vision, cognition, biomedical informatics, robotics, information networks, human-robot interactions, computational sustainability *AI technical components*: Fisher's exact test, inductive reasoning, nearest neighbor algorithm, correlation, graph search algorithms, computational game theory, optimization, agent-based modeling, probabilistic reasoning *AI literacy*: Understanding how ML works, the process behind creating ML models, and the ability to reflect on its personal and societal implications	Kaspersen et al. (2021b); Kahn et al. (2018); Zhang & Du (2008)

Based on the P21's Framework for the 21st Century Learning, this section discusses the potential of adding AI literacy to map different components of the framework (see Fig. 4.4). The P21's Framework lists three types of skills: learning and innovation skills (creativity, critical thinking and problem-solving, communication and collaboration), literacy skills (information, media, and ICT literacy), and life skills (flexibility and adaptability, initiative and self-direction, social and cross-cultural skills, productivity and accountability, and leadership and responsibility) that are required in core subjects and twenty-first century themes.

Information, Media, and Technology Skills The twenty-first century skills cover digital literacies, and AI literacy belongs to one of the digital literacy skills. There are various information and technological skills involved when learning AI. First, students can accomplish learning tasks in an AI-driven environment. Students learn the characteristics of AI-empowered devices and applications to make use of them in their day-to-day activities. Moreover, various AI systems such as recommendation systems, intelligent agents, and advanced AI algorithms can help people facili-

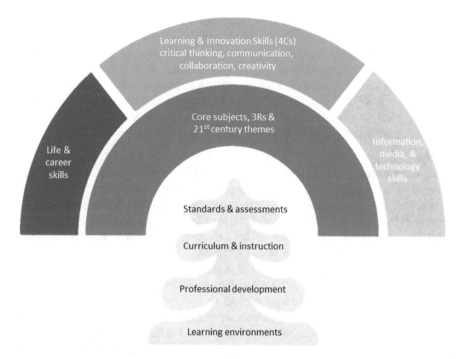

Fig. 4.4 AI literacy as a twenty-first century skill

tate information search and retrieval. Students can also critically judge the usefulness and sufficiency of AI-generated advice and information. Furthermore, various social media platforms use AI to analyze key moments in photos and live videos which make users more personalized and customized resulting in higher engagement (Vale & Fernandes, 2018). AI can also help automate video creation and adjust their video contents and elements seamlessly (e.g., colors, audio tracks, video) and speed up their editing process using mobile devices. AI tools can help interact with users and customers to enhance their user experience.

Learning and Innovation Skills   The skill sets (or the 4 Cs) of twenty-first century learning include (1) critical thinking and problem-solving, (2) creativity and innovation, (3) communication, and (4) collaboration. First, AI literates can use appropriate AI applications to solve authentic problems and make critical decisions. In Yoder et al. (2020)'s study, students were asked to utilize particular AI algorithms and leverage-related techniques to solve real-world problems such as building a contact tracing application for the pandemic. Another study conducted by Long and Magerko (2020) encouraged students to collaboratively create music together using AI-generated music machines through changing parameters.

Communication requires students to transmit ideas, information, and knowledge with others effectively using a variety of AI tools (e.g., chat bots, diagnostic evaluation). Huo (2019) proposed an online diagnosis evaluation program to assist secondary students to improve their English presentations. A diagnostic evaluation of presentation skills can help students examine their strengths and weaknesses, presentation content, style, and length to optimize their communication. On a higher-level application of AI, some studies have tried to incorporate these elements as important curriculum standards to cultivate AI and computational thinking (Deng et al., 2021).

Life and Career Skills   AI literacy is more than technological understanding which should involve a range of critical, reflective, and social perspectives (Gut, 2011). Therefore, skill sets such as ethical awareness, flexibility and adaptability, initiative and self-direction, cultural awareness, lifelong learning, productivity and accountability, and leadership and responsibility are important to enhance students' competitiveness and capacity in our global knowledge economy. First, students should learn AI-related awareness and knowledge about legal and ethical aspects. Several key components (e.g., fairness, responsibility, transparency, trust) were identified in prior studies to learn about the legal, ethical, and cultural concerns of personally and socially responsible use of AI. Students should understand the potential risks and evaluate the impact of AI in social, economic, and cultural contexts (Hagendorff, 2020). Moreover, since AI literacy is important for today's digital era, students have to adapt to such AI digital transformation and get ready for the future workforce. Other contextual twenty-first century skills (e.g., self-direction, flexibility, lifelong learning) are also vital for students to adapt to their thinking and attitude to the fast-changing society, managing learning progression toward these goals, and exploring new opportunities when using AI (Goralski & Tan, 2020). In other words, students are not only end users of AI technologies who know the basic concepts behind. They will grow up to become responsible citizens who know how to use AI and work with AI to make people and our society a better place to live in.

Core Subjects: 3Rs and Twenty-First Century Themes   To prepare students to be successful in the future, students are required to master the core subjects and twenty-first century themes. In fact, AI has been incorporated across subject knowledge (e.g., language, arts, mathematics, economics, science) and other twenty-first century themes (i.e., global awareness, environmental, financial, civic, and health literacy). Educators can discuss how AI influences our everyday life and industries. For example, in language education, Zhang (2018) developed young learners' AI literacy through interacting with an AI-empowered robot to practice English speaking. Moreover, students can learn the potential of using machine learning to help disease prediction and diagnosis and facilitate treatment effectiveness and drug discovery (Noorbakhsh-Sabet et al., 2019). It is meaningful to engage students in expressing knowledge from other disciplines and equip them with insights into AI-empowered modeling, data analysis, and problem-solving such as predicting the quality of mangoes in STEM education (Sakulkueakulsuk et al., 2018), using drones to help traffic management (Lundberg et al., 2018) and practice AI and computational thinking in mathematics education (Tamborg et al., 2022).

To summarize, through integrating three essential AI digital competencies (i.e., (1) information, media and technology skills; (2) learning and innovation skills; and (3) life and career skills), into different core subjects, this section helps establish a conceptual twenty-first century skills framework and propose different digital skill dimensions by evaluating research articles that define the skill sets. It has resulted in a framework of core skills including technical, information skills, communication, collaboration, creativity, critical thinking and problem-solving, as well as other contextual skills such as ethical awareness, cultural awareness, flexibility, self-direction, and lifelong learning. This framework informs policymakers to meet the educational standards in their countries/regions and provides related professional development for educators to move forward. The framework also serves as a basis of educational reform and digital transformation across educational institutions. In a fast-changing knowledge economy, these skills bring learning opportunities for students to enhance their competitiveness and capacity to drive innovation, develop twenty-first century literacy skills to cope in this changing society, and fulfill the job demands. AI literacy education is still in its infancy stage, and the existing research papers are not mature enough to uncover all necessary skills at our ever-changing times. As such, this section is suggestive that AI literacy plays an increasingly important role as part of the twenty-first-century digital skills. A more detailed structure and operational instructions on incorporating this notion require further exploration.

4.6   Conclusion

In recent 5 years, countries/regions and K–16 educational institutions have started to design related policies, curricula, and learning programs to promote AI literacy for students. We start to see educational frameworks that emerge in supporting the habitat for AI literacy education to blossom (e.g., Long & Magerko, 2020; AIK12, 2022). Other scholars also wrote review articles to summarize the important findings. They identified certain technologies, learning content, pedagogy, and educational standards to be appropriate for AI literacy education. By our research team, a scoping review was also conducted to give an overview of AI literacy education implemented from 2016 to 2021.

This chapter examined how AI literacy interacts with twenty-first century skills by looking through the lens of three proposed educational models (i.e., Bloom, TPACK, and P21). The results demonstrated the use of Bloom's taxonomy to view cognition levels of AI literacy education, TPACK model to understand how educators should learn to equip their students with AI literacy, and the P21's Framework to identify the four types of digital competences in the twenty-first century. As suggested by the UNESCO (2022, p. 61), "all citizens need to be equipped with some level of AI literacy covering the values, knowledge and skills relating to AI." However, there is a lack of studies investigating what and how to teach AI at a specific educational level. The results in this chapter can formulate a theoretical basis for us to further investigate how AI literacy can and should be conducted at each educational level. Our proposal serves as guidelines to define what K–16 students should know about AI and assist different stakeholders (e.g., curriculum designers, AI developers, policymakers) to learn the standards of essential AI knowledge, skills, attitudes, values, and ethics across grade bands.

References

AIK12. (2022) *Grade band progression chats.* Retrieved from https://ai4k12.org/gradeband-progression-charts/

Bruce, C. (1997). *The seven faces of information literacy.* Auslib Press, Adelaide, South Australia. Retrieved from https://eprints.qut.edu.au/139611/.

Burgsteiner, H., Kandlhofer, M., & Steinbauer, G. (2016, March). Irobot: Teaching the basics of artificial intelligence in high schools. In *Proceedings of the AAAI Conference on Artificial Intelligence* (Vol. 30, No. 1).

Celik, I. (2022). Towards intelligent-TPACK: An empirical study on teachers' professional knowledge to ethically integrate artificial intelligence (AI)-based tools into education. *Computers in Human Behavior, 138,* 107468.

Chai, C. S., Lin, P. Y., Jong, M. S. Y., Dai, Y., Chiu, T. K., & Qin, J. (2021). Perceptions of and behavioral intentions towards learning artificial intelligence in primary school students. *Educational Technology & Society, 24*(3), 89–101.

Chan, K. S., & Zary, N. (2019). Applications and challenges of implementing artificial intelligence in medical education: Integrative review. *JMIR Medical Education, 5*(1), e13930.

Chiu, T. K., Meng, H., Chai, C. S., King, I., Wong, S., & Yam, Y. (2021). Creation and evaluation of a pretertiary artificial intelligence (AI) curriculum. *IEEE Transactions on Education, 65*(1), 30–39.

Chu, S. K. W., Reynolds, R. B., Tavares, N. J., Notari, M., & Lee, C. W. Y. (2021). *21st century skills development through inquiry-based learning from theory to practice.* Springer International Publishing.

CSET. (2021). *AI education in China and the United States.* Retrieved from https://cset.georgetown.edu/wpcontent/uploads/CSET-AI-Education-in-China-and-the-United-States-1.pdf

Demeshkant, N., Potyrala, K., & Tomczyk, L. (2020). Levels of academic teachers digital competence: Polish case-study. In *2020 Proceedings of the 28th International Conference on Computers in Education* (pp. 591–601).

Deng, W., Huang, X., Liu, Q., & Wang, Z. (2021). Curriculum design of artificial intelligence in middle school – Taking posture recognition as an example. In *2021 tenth international conference of educational innovation through technology* (pp. 310–315).

Dignum, V. (2019). *Responsible artificial intelligence: How to develop and use AI in a responsible way.* Springer.

Druga, S., Vu, S. T., Likhith, E., & Qiu, T. (2019). Inclusive AI literacy for kids around the world. In *Proceedings of FabLearn 2019* (pp. 104–111).

Estevez, J., Garate, G., & Graña, M. (2019). Gentle introduction to artificial intelligence for high-school students using scratch. *IEEE Access, 7,* 179027–179036.

Fernández-Martínez, C., Hernán-Losada, I., & Fernández, A. (2021). Early introduction of AI in Spanish Middle Schools. A motivational study. *KI-Künstliche Intelligenz, 35*(2), 163–170.

Fleaca, E., & Stanciu, R. D. (2019). Digital-age learning and business engineering education–A pilot study on students' E-skills. *Procedia Manufacturing, 32*, 1051–1057.

Gamire, E., & Pearson, G. (Eds.). (2006). *Tech tally: Approaches to assessing technological literacy*. Island Press.

Goel, A. (2017). AI education for the world. *AI Magazine, 38*(2), 3–4.

Gong, X., Tang, Y., Liu, X., Jing, S., Cui, W., Liang, J., & Wang, F. Y. (2020, October). K-9 artificial intelligence education in Qingdao: Issues, challenges and suggestions. In *2020 IEEE International Conference on Networking, Sensing and Control (ICNSC)* (pp. 1–6). IEEE.

Goralski, M. A., & Tan, T. K. (2020). Artificial intelligence and sustainable development. *The International Journal of Management Education, 18*(1), 100330.

Gresse von Wangenheim, C., Hauck, J. C., Pacheco, F. S., & Bertonceli Bueno, M. F. (2021). Visual tools for teaching machine learning in K-12: A ten-year systematic mapping. *Education and Information Technologies, 26*(5), 5733–5778.

Gunasilan, U. (2021). Debate as a learning activity for teaching programming: A case in the subject of machine learning. *Higher Education, Skills and Work-Based Learning, 12*(4), 705–718.

Gut, D. M. (2011). Integrating 21st century skills into the curriculum. In *Bringing schools into the 21st century* (pp. 137–157). Springer.

Hagendorff, T. (2020). The ethics of AI ethics: An evaluation of guidelines. *Minds and Machines, 30*(1), 99–120.

Han, E. R., Yeo, S., Kim, M. J., Lee, Y. H., Park, K. H., & Roh, H. (2019). Medical education trends for future physicians in the era of advanced technology and artificial intelligence: An integrative review. *BMC Medical Education, 19*(1), 1–15.

Heinze, C. A., Haase, J., & Higgins, H. (2010, July). An action research report from a multi-year approach to teaching artificial intelligence at the k-6 level. *First AAAI Symposium on Educational Advances in Artificial Intelligence, 24*, 1890–1895.

How, M. L., & Hung, W. L. D. (2019). Educing AI-thinking in science, technology, engineering, arts, and mathematics (STEAM) education. *Education Sciences, 9*(3), 184.

Huitt, W. (2011). Bloom et al.'s taxonomy of the cognitive domain. *Educational Psychology Interactive, 22*, 1–4.

Huo, Y. (2019). Analysis of intelligent evaluation algorithm based on English diagnostic system. *Cluster Computing, 22*(6), 13821–13826.

Janssen, C., Segers, E., McQueen, J. M., & Verhoeven, L. (2019). Comparing effects of instruction on word meaning and word form on early literacy abilities in kindergarten. *Early Education and Development, 30*(3), 375–399.

Julie, H., Alyson, H., & Anne-Sophie, C. (2020, October). Designing digital literacy activities: An interdisciplinary and collaborative approach. In *2020 IEEE Frontiers in Education Conference (FIE)* (pp. 1–5). IEEE.

Kahn, K. M., Megasari, R., Piantari, E., & Junaeti, E. (2018). *AI programming by children using snap! Block programming in a developing country*. Retrieved from https://ora.ox.ac.uk/objects/uuid:9a82b522-6f9f-4c67-b20dbe6c53019b3b

Kandlhofer, M., Steinbauer, G., Hirschmugl-Gaisch, S., & Huber, P. (2016, October). Artificial intelligence and computer science in education: From kindergarten to university. In *2016 IEEE Frontiers in Education Conference (FIE)* (pp. 1–9). IEEE.

Kaspersen, M. H., Bilstrup, K. E. K., & Petersen, M. G. (2021a, February). The machine learning machine: A tangible user interface for teaching machine learning. In *Proceedings of the fifteenth international conference on Tangible, Embedded, and Embodied Interaction* (pp. 1–12).

Kaspersen, M. H., Bilstrup, K. E. K., Van Mechelen, M., Hjorth, A., Bouvin, N. O., & Petersen, M. G. (2021b, June). VotestratesML: A high school learning tool for exploring machine learning and its societal implications. In *FabLearn Europe/MakeEd 2021-An international conference on computing, design and making in education* (pp.1–10).

Kim, S., Jang, Y., Kim, W., Choi, S., Jung, H., Kim, S., & Kim, H. (2021, May). Why and what to teach: AI curriculum for elementary school. In *Proceedings of the AAAI Conference on Artificial Intelligence* (Vol. 35, No. 17, pp. 15569–15576).

Koehler, M. J., Mishra, P., & Cain, W. (2013). What is technological pedagogical content knowl-edge (TPACK)? *Journal of Education, 193*(3), 13–19.

Kong, S. C., Cheung, W. M. Y., & Zhang, G. (2021). Evaluation of an artificial intelligence literacy course for university students with diverse study backgrounds. *Computers and Education: Artificial Intelligence, 2*, 100026.

Kokotsaki, D., Menzies, V., & Wiggins, A. (2016). Project-based learning: A review of the litera-ture. *Improving Schools, 19*(3), 267–277.

Lao, N. (2020). *Reorienting machine learning education towards tinkerers and ML-engaged citi-zens.* Massachusetts Institute of Technology.

Lee, I., Ali, S., Zhang, H., DiPaola, D., & Breazeal, C. (2021, March). Developing middle school Students' AI literacy. In *Proceedings of the 52nd ACM Technical Symposium on Computer Science Education* (pp. 191–197).

Lin, P., & Van Brummelen, J. (2021, May). Engaging teachers to co-design integrated AI curricu-lum for K-12 classrooms. In *Proceedings of the 2021 CHI Conference on Human Factors in Computing Systems* (pp. 1–12).

Livingstone, S. (2004). Media literacy and the challenge of new information and communication technologies. *The Communication Review, 7*(1), 3–14.

Long, D., & Magerko, B. (2020, April). What is AI literacy? Competencies and design consider-ations. In *Proceedings of the 2020 CHI Conference on Human Factors in Computing Systems* (pp. 1–16).

Lundberg, J., Arvola, M., Westin, C., Holmlid, S., Nordvall, M., & Josefsson, B. (2018). Cognitive work analysis in the conceptual design of first-of-a-kind systems–designing urban air traffic management. *Behaviour & Information Technology, 37*(9), 904–925.

McCarthy, J. (2007). From here to human-level AI. *Artificial Intelligence, 171*(18), 1174–1182.

Microsoft News Center India. (2022). *Empowering India to be future ready.* Retrieved from https://news.microsoft.com/en-in/

MIT (2021). *RAISE- Responsible AI for Social Empowerment and Education.* Retrieved from https://raise.mit.edu/

Morris, T. H. (2020). Experiential learning–a systematic review and revision of Kolb's model. *Interactive Learning Environments, 28*(8), 1064–1077.

Narahara, T., & Kobayashi, Y. (2018). Personalizing homemade bots with plug & play AI for STEAM education. In *SIGGRAPH Asia 2018 technical briefs* (pp. 1–4).

National Research Council. (2012). *Education for life and work: Developing transferable knowl-edge and skills in the 21st century.* National Academies Press.

Ng, D. T. K., & Chu, S. K. W. (2021). Motivating students to learn AI through social networking sites: A case study in Hong Kong. *Online Learning, 25*(1), 195–208.

Ng, D.T.K., Lai, L.F.W., & Cheung T.W.T. (2021). Artificial Intelligence for All. eFunLearning Ltd., Hong Kong Science and Technology Parks, Hong Kong.

Ng, D. T. K., Leung, J. K. L., Chu, K. W. S., & Qiao, M. S. (2021). AI literacy: Definition, teach-ing, evaluation and ethical issues. *Proceedings of the Association for Information Science and Technology, 58*(1), 504–509.

Ng, D. T. K., Luo, W., Chan, H. M. Y., & Chu, S. K. W. (2022). Using digital story writing as a pedagogy to develop AI literacy among primary students. *Computers and Education: Artificial Intelligence, 3*, 100054.

Noorbakhsh-Sabet, N., Zand, R., Zhang, Y., & Abedi, V. (2019). Artificial intelligence transforms the future of health care. *The American Journal of Medicine, 132*(7), 795–801.

Reyes, M., Meier, R., Pereira, S., Silva, C. A., Dahlweid, F. M., Tengg-Kobligk, H. V., et al. (2020). On the interpretability of artificial intelligence in radiology: Challenges and opportunities. *Radiology: Artificial Intelligence, 2*(3), e190043.

Riina, V., Stefano, K., & Yves, P. (2022). *DigComp 2.2: The digital competence framework for citizens – With new examples of knowledge, skills and attitudes.* Retrieved from https://publica-tions.jrc.ec.europa.eu/repository/handle/JRC128415

Robinson, S., Orsingher, C., Alkire, L., De Keyser, A., Giebelhausen, M., Papamichail, K. N., et al. (2020). Frontline encounters of the AI kind: An evolved service encounter framework. *Journal of Business Research, 116*, 366–376.

Rodríguez-García, J. D., Moreno-León, J., Román-González, M., & Robles, G. (2020, October). Introducing artificial intelligence fundamentals with LearningML: Artificial intelligence made easy. In *Eighth International Conference on Technological Ecosystems for Enhancing Multiculturality* (pp. 18–20).

Roll, I., & Wylie, R. (2016). Evolution and revolution in artificial intelligence in education. *International Journal of Artificial Intelligence in Education, 26*(2), 582–599.

Sabuncuoglu, A. (2020, June). Designing one year curriculum to teach artificial intelligence for middle school. In *Proceedings of the 2020 ACM Conference on Innovation and Technology in Computer Science Education* (pp. 96–102).

Sakulkueakulsuk, B., Witoon, S., Ngarmkajornwiwat, P., Pataranutaporn, P., Surareungchai, W., Pataranutaporn, P., & Subsoontorn, P. (2018, December). Kids making AI: Integrating machine learning, gamification, and social context in STEM education. In *2018 IEEE International Conference on Teaching, Assessment, and Learning for Engineering (TALE)* (pp. 1005–1010). IEEE.

Sanusi, I. T., Olaleye, S. A., Agbo, F. J., & Chiu, T. K. (2022). The role of learners' competencies in artificial intelligence education. *Computers and Education: Artificial Intelligence, 3*, 100098.

Sing, C. C., Teo, T., Huang, F., & Chiu, T. K. (2022). Secondary school students' intentions to learn AI: Testing moderation effects of readiness, social good and optimism. *Educational Technology Research and Development, 70*(3), 765–782.

Steinbauer, G., Kandlhofer, M., Chklovski, T., Heintz, F., & Koenig, S. (2021). A differentiated discussion about AI education K-12. *KI-Künstliche Intelligenz, 35*(2), 131–137.

Su, J., Zhong, Y., & Ng, D. T. K. (2022). *A meta-review of literature on educational approaches for teaching AI at the K-12 levels in the Asia-Pacific region* (p. 100065). Artificial Intelligence.

Talja, S., Tuominen, K., & Savolainen, R. (2005). *"Isms" in information science: Constructivism, collectivism and constructionism. Journal of Documentation* (Vol. 61, pp. 79–101).

Tamborg, A. L., Jankvist, U. T., & Misfeldt, M. (2022). Comparing programing and computational thinking with mathematical digital competencies form an implementation perspective. In *Proceedings of the 15th International Conference on Technology in Mathematics Teaching (ICTMT 15)* (p. 298). Danish School of Education, Aarhus University.

Tedre, M., Toivonen, T., Kahila, J., Vartiainen, H., Valtonen, T., Jormanainen, I., & Pears, A. (2021). Teaching machine learning in K–12 classroom: Pedagogical and technological trajectories for artificial intelligence education. *IEEE Access, 9*, 110558–110572.

Touretzky, D., Gardner-McCune, C., Martin, F., & Seehorn, D. (2019). Envisioning AI for K-12: What should every child know about AI? *Proceedings of the AAAI Conference on Artificial Intelligence, 33*(1), 9795–9799.

Touretzky, D., Gardner-McCune, C., & Seehorn, D. (2022). Machine Learning and the Five Big Ideas in AI. *International Journal of Artificial Intelligence in Education*, 1–34.

UNESCO. (2018). *A global framework of reference on digital literacy skills for indicator 4.4.2.* Retrieved from https://uis.unesco.org/sites/default/files/documents/ip51-global-framework-reference-digital-literacy-skills-2018-en.pdf

UNESCO. (2022). *K-12 AI curricula A mapping of government-endorsed AI curricula.* Retrieved from https://unesdoc.unesco.org/ark:/48223/pf0000380602.

Vachovsky, M. E., Wu, G., Chaturapruek, S., Russakovsky, O., Sommer, R., & Fei-Fei, L. (2016, February). Toward more gender diversity in CS through an artificial intelligence summer program for high school girls. In *Proceedings of the 47th ACM technical symposium on Computing Science Education* (pp. 303–308).

Vale, L., & Fernandes, T. (2018). Social media and sports: Driving fan engagement with football clubs on Facebook. *Journal of Strategic Marketing, 26*(1), 37–55.

Van Laar, E., Van Deursen, A. J., Van Dijk, J. A., & De Haan, J. (2017). The relation between 21st-century skills and digital skills: A systematic literature review. *Computers in Human Behavior, 72*, 577–588.

Vazhayil, A., Shetty, R., Bhavani, R. R., & Akshay, N. (2019, December). Focusing on teacher education to introduce AI in schools: Perspectives and illustrative findings. In *2019 IEEE Tenth International Conference on Technology for Education (T4E)* (pp. 71–77). IEEE.

Wan, X., Zhou, X., Ye, Z., Mortensen, C. K., & Bai, Z. (2020, June). SmileyCluster: Supporting accessible machine learning in K-12 scientific discovery. In *Proceedings of the Interaction Design and Children Conference* (pp. 23–35).

Wang, T., & Cheng, E. C. K. (2021). An investigation of barriers to Hong Kong K-12 schools incorporating artificial intelligence in education. *Computers and Education: Artificial Intelligence, 2*, 100031.

Williams, R., Park, H. W., Oh, L., & Breazeal, C. (2019). Popbots: Designing an artificial intelligence curriculum for early childhood education. *Proceedings of the AAAI Conference on Artificial Intelligence, 33*(01), 9729–9736.

Wong, G. K., Ma, X., Dillenbourg, P., & Huan, J. (2020). Broadening artificial intelligence education in K-12: Where to start? *ACM Inroads, 11*(1), 20–29.

Xia, Q., Chiu, T. K., Lee, M., Sanusi, I. T., Dai, Y., & Chai, C. S. (2022). A self-determination theory (SDT) design approach for inclusive and diverse artificial intelligence (AI) education. *Computers & Education, 189*, 104582.

Yau, K. W., Chai, C. S., Chiu, T. K., Meng, H., King, I., & Yam, Y. (2022). A phenomenographic approach on teacher conceptions of teaching artificial intelligence (AI) in K-12 schools. *Education and Information Technologies*, 1–24.

Yoder, S., Tatar, C., Aderemi, I., Boorugu, S., Jiang, S., & Akram, B. (2020). Gaining insight into effective teaching of AI problem-solving through CSEDM: A case study. In *5th Workshop on Computer Science Educational Data Mining*.

Zhang, Z. (2018, February). Develop the AI literacy of infants by deeply integrated English learning and robot education. In *2018 International Conference on Computer Science, Electronics and Communication Engineering (CSECE 2018)* (pp. 154–156). Atlantis Press.

Zhang, J., & Du, H. (2008, December). The PBL's application research on Prolog Language's Instruction. In *2008 international workshop on education technology and training & 2008 international workshop on geoscience and remote sensing* (Vol. 1, pp. 112–114). IEEE.

Zimmermann-Niefield, A., Turner, M., Murphy, B., Kane, S. K., & Shapiro, R. B. (2019, June). Youth learning machine learning through building models of athletic moves. In *Proceedings of the 18th ACM international conference on interaction design and children* (pp. 121–132).

Part II
K-16 AI Literacy Education

Chapter 5
AI Literacy Education in Early Childhood Education

Part I of this book gave us basic ideas about what AI literacy is, why it is important for all K–16 learners, as well as the theoretical frameworks and important theories involved in AI literacy education. However, students at each educational level have varied needs and intended learning outcomes. Therefore, the way of how AI literacy education is being implemented across levels of education should not be the same. Identifying specific age-appropriate approaches on different educational levels could inform schools, policymakers, educators, and parents on the design and development of adequate environment, pedagogy, learning content, technology, and assessment tools that best meet the needs of their students.

Part II of this book further gives us an outline of AI literacy education across educational levels. Several models of AI literacy education, in particular Bloom's taxonomy and the TPACK model, comprise key digital competencies to inform K–16 educators what knowledge, skills, and attitudes students should equip with. The following three chapters will first explain the research method including literature search and data analysis. After that, we conduct a systematic scoping review on four research questions and discuss the findings based on the TPACK model for each educational level:

• What pedagogical strategies were commonly used in AI literacy studies?
• What learning content is appropriate for students in AI literacy studies?
• What learning tools have been used in AI literacy studies?
• What assessment methods have been used in AI literacy studies?

5.1 Introduction

Most AI literacy research was conducted in primary, secondary, and higher education settings (Eguchi et al., 2021; Su et al., 2022). However, much less attention has been paid to how AI education for young children aged 3–8 years relative to other age groups. Early childhood education refers to the education and care of children from birth up to 8 years of age. Although previous studies have brought AI learning tools into early childhood education classrooms and shown their promising effects (e.g., Williams et al., 2019a; Lin et al., 2020; Tseng et al., 2021), very little has been known about the AI literacy for early childhood education.

Artificial intelligence literacy education can be started as young as kindergarteners. As suggested in Chap. 3, not only AI literacy helps young children to develop adequate technological literacy that positively influence their living and future study; it effectively develops many other skills for their cognitive development, such as computational thinking, theory of mind skills, inquiry skills, emotional literacy, and collaboration (Su & Yang, 2022; Williams et al., 2019a, b; Kewalramani et al., 2021). For example, Kewalramani et al. (2021) designed a set of AI learning activities for 4 to 5-year-old children to play and interact with AI toys to enhance their three types of literacies including creating inquiry literacy, emotional inquiry literacy, and collaborative inquiry literacy. Another study conducted by Druga et al. (2019) designed an AI-interfaced robot for children in order to teach them about the capabilities of AI agents. Therefore, it is meaningful to systematically analyze and discuss existing work focusing on AI literacy in early childhood education (ECE) development. Four research questions (RQ) formed the basis of this section:

RQ1: What are the pedagogical strategies used in AI literacy studies at the ECE level?
RQ2: What learning content is appropriate in AI literacy studies at the ECE level?
RQ3: What learning tools have been used in AI literacy studies at the ECE level?
RQ4: What assessment methods have been used in AI literacy studies at the ECE level?

5.2 Methods

This chapter followed the procedures for the *Preferred Reporting Items for Systematic Reviews and Meta-Analyses* the PRISMA statement (Moher et al., 2009). In order to facilitate database search, this study surveyed peer-reviewed academic articles published in all years. All articles were accessed in June 2022. Databases searched were Web of Science, IEEE, and Scopus. We formulated a search string based on our understanding of and knowledge in the AI education domain and also by referring to related AI education search strings used in other studies such as Su and Yang (2022). The search string used for this study was "artificial intelligence" OR "AI" OR "machine learning" OR "ML" AND "early childhood" OR "young child*" OR "preschool*" OR "kindergarten*" OR "pre-k*" OR "childcare" OR "child care" OR "day-care" OR "children" AND "curricula*" OR "learning" OR "curriculum design." As a result, a total of 3474 articles were retrieved, among which 142 were from Web of Science, 3042 from Scopus, and 299 from IEEE.

First, by reading through their title and abstract, 3389 results were excluded due to their irrelevance to the research topic. Second, 18 results were excluded that reported duplicate studies. Then, by closely examining their full text, we excluded the articles (a) in which participants were not 3–8 years old (15), (b) that focus was not AI or machine learning (ML) (11), and (c) that did not discuss curriculum design or learning programs/activities (26). Eligible studies included in this review were restricted to articles written in the English language. After considering the articles based on the criteria, 15 studies remained. Figure 5.1 below provides an overview of our search protocol.

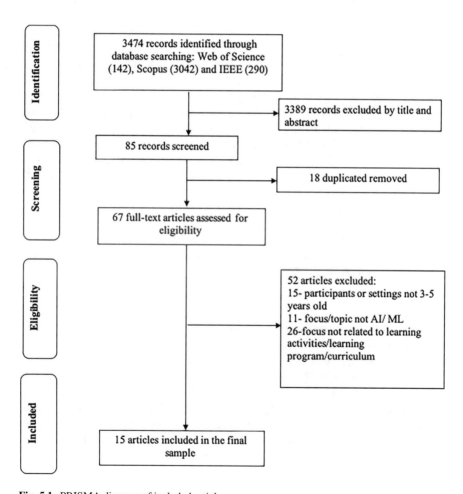

Fig. 5.1 PRISMA diagram of included articles

5.3   Results and Discussion

Fifteen articles that focused on AI literacy in early childhood education were thoroughly examined in this review (Table 5.1). Different types of literature are included in this review, such as research articles and conference papers. Fifteen articles that focused on AI literacy in early childhood education were thoroughly reviewed (2016, 1 article; 2018, 1 article; 2019, 3 articles; 2020, 2 articles; 2021, 4 articles, and 2022, 4 articles). To facilitate the database search, this study identifies all peer-reviewed academic articles published from 2018 to 2021 since the first article was found in 2016 (Kandlhofer et al., 2016). This review shows that all studies were conducted in developed countries/regions (e.g., the United States, Austria, Germany, Denmark, Sweden, Japan, Hong Kong, and Australia).

RQ1: What Were the Pedagogical Strategies Commonly Used in AI Early Childhood Education Studies?
In terms of the pedagogical strategies design used, most studies were very successful. To begin with, the pedagogical strategies include learning activities, learning methods, and AI learning tools. Most researchers in the AI in early childhood education field have developed learning programs designed to improve children's AI-related knowledge, such as AI concepts, knowledge-based systems, supervised machine learning, generative AI, machine learning and data science, and AI and ethics (e.g., Kandlhofer et al., 2016; Williams et al., 2019a, b; Lin et al., 2020; Tseng et al., 2021). Second, one study used methods of discovery- and inquiry-based learning, storytelling, and educational robotics to teach different AI and computer science topics to children (Kandlhofer et al., 2016). Third, three popular AI tools, such as PopBots (Williams, 2018; Williams et al., 2019a, b), Zhorai (Lin et al., 2020), and PlushPal (Tseng et al., 2021) designed an AI and machine learning curriculum for children, helping children in better understanding the concept or knowledge of AI or machine learning (Lin et al., 2020; Williams et al., 2019a, b; Tseng et al., 2021). Lastly, six children explored machine learning based technology in nonschool settings (Vartiainen et al., 2020).

RQ2: What Learning Contents Are Appropriate for Students at the ECE Level?
Different AI learning contents are included in ECE level, such as rule-based systems, supervised learning, generative AI, and machine learning (e.g., Lin et al., 2020; Su & Zhong, 2022; Williams, 2018). For example, Su and Zhong (2022) designed an AI curriculum framework in ECE settings; the learning contents include definition of AI and examples of AI, the five big ideas in AI, machine learning, applications, and AI ethics (Table 5.2). This study also designed some learning activities to enhance children's AI tools skill (Su & Zhong, 2022). For example, Su and Zhong (2022) designed Google's Quick, Draw! activities to enhance children's use of AI tools skill.

Table 5.1 Descriptive information of the included studies

Author/year	Research methods	Pedagogical strategies	Learning content	Learning tools	Assessment methods
Lin et al. (2020)	Quantitative	/	What does Zhorai know Teaching Zhorai Witnessing machine learning AI and ethics	Zhorai	Knowledge assessments (pre- and post-assessments)
Kandlhofer et al. (2016)	Qualitative	Discovery- and inquiry-based learning, storytelling, and educational robotics	AI/computer science topic	/	Video data, pictures and observations (field notes)
Williams (2018)	Quantitative	Creative design activities: draw the AI robots Real-world AI activities: Google quick draw	Rule-based systems Supervised machine learning, and generative AI	PopBots	Theory of mind assessment, rock paper scissors assessment performance, supervised learning assessment performance, generative assessment performance, pre- and posttests of children's perception, attitudes assessment
Williams et al. (2019a)	Quantitative	AI activities Introduction to programming with the PopBotsKnowledge-based systems with rock-paper-scissors; supervised machine learning with food classification; generative AI with music remix	Knowledge-based systems, supervised machine learning, and generative AI	PopBots	PopBots assessment, theory of mind assessment, and perception of robots questionnaire

(continued)

Table 5.1 (continued)

Author/year	Research methods	Pedagogical strategies	Learning content	Learning tools	Assessment methods
Williams et al. (2019b)	Quantitative	Knowledge-based systems with rock-paper-scissors Supervised machine learning with food; generative AI with music remix	Knowledge-based systems, supervised machine learning, and generative music AI	PopBots	Pre- and post-assessments (knowledge)
Druga et al. (2019)	Quantitative	Interact with AI agents; AI perception monster game	AI perception and expectations	Jibo robot, Anki's Cozmo robot and Amazon's Alexa	AI perception questionnaire
Dwivedi (2021)	Mixed	The design activity: Teachable Machine	Machine learning concepts	Teachable Machine	Machine learning metric and training data
Druga and Ko (2021)	Mixed	Learning activities: "Make me happy program", "rock paper scissors program", "smart home program"	Cognimates AI platform (train, code and test a series of smart programs)	Cognimates AI platform	Pre-/ post-perception game responses and observations
Tseng et al. (2021)	Quantitative	Created a project using three common gestures, such as none, jump, and running	The fundamentals of machine learning and data science	PlushPal	Surveys
Kewalramani et al. (2021)	Qualitative	Playing with battery-operated robots (Botley and Beebots) and using block play to build ramps and roadways for their robots to travel	/	Cozmo Blue Bot Coji by Wowee, Qobo the snail, and vernie-Lego boost bot	Interviews and observations

(continued)

Table 5.1 (continued)

Author/year	Research methods	Pedagogical strategies	Learning content	Learning tools	Assessment methods
Druga et al. (2022a)	Qualitative	Activity: Classification game; anchor game; reflection; object recognition; train AI; prediction game; compare with voice assistant; draw what is inside; AI bingo game; analyze AI; design AI	Image classification; Object recognition Voice assistants Unplugged AI games and co-design Reflection on study and learning activities	Teachable Machine	Video recording: transcribed the videos and noted comments
Yang (2022)	/	AI + ocean protection	Machine learning	Popbo Clearbot	/
Vartiainen et al. (2020)	Qualitative	/	Explore the input-output relationships with GTM	Google's Teachable Machine	Video data
Su and Zhong (2022)	/	Problem-based learning: AI farming	Module: Introduction to AI Module 2: Machine learning Module 3: Speech recognition Module 4: Flaws and biases of AI	PictoBlox	/
Tazume et al. (2021)	/	Play with AI robots	/	RoBoHoN	/

Table 5.2 AI curriculum for ECE

AI knowledge	AI skills	AI attitudes
K1: Definition of AI and examples of AI	S1: Using AI tools	A1: Social impact
K2: The five big ideas in AI	S2: Computational thinking and programming	A2: Collaborate with AI
K3: Machine learning	S3: Critical thinking	
K4: Applications	S4: Problem-solving	
K5: AI ethics		

Adopted from Su and Zhong (2022)

RQ3: What Were the Learning Tools Used in AI Early Childhood Education?
As shown in Table 5.3, three studies have used PopBots and Teachable Machines as the learning tools for supporting children's engagement in AI. Other AI learning tools reported in the studies include Zhorai, Jibo robot, Anki's Cozmo robot, Amazon's Alexa, Cognimates AI platform, PlushPal, Popbo, Clearbot, RoBoHoN, and PictoBlox. These learning tools seem to enhance children's learning AI concepts. For example, children understand three AI concepts (knowledge-based systems, supervised machine learning, and generative music) using AI learning tools (i.e., PopBots) (Williams, 2018; Williams et al., 2019a, b).

RQ4: What Assessment Methods Have Been Used in Researching AI in Early Childhood Education?
Most studies used a quantitative design and mixed-method design, followed by the qualitative design. Of note is that three articles (Su & Zhong, 2022; Yang, 2022; Tazume et al., 2021) only introduced and described their AI curricula in early childhood education, without implementing them in practice, and thus no data was collected. More details are shown in Fig. 5.2.

In terms of assessment methods, knowledge assessments/tests (4) are the most commonly used, followed by robot-based assessment and video analysis (3), as shown in Table 5.4. Four studies used knowledge assessments to assess children's AI understandings (Lin et al., 2020; Williams, 2018; Williams et al., 2019a, b) (see Table 5.1). For example, some scholars used knowledge tests to examine children's machine learning knowledge using Zhorai (Lin et al., 2020). According to the results, Zhorai can help children understand machine learning concepts more easily.

Table 5.3 Learning tools

Learning tools	Website
PopBots	https://www.media.mit.edu/projects/pop-kit/overview/
Teachable Machine	https://teachablemachine.withgoogle.com/
Zhorai	http://zhorai.csail.mit.edu/
Jobo robot	https://jibo.com/
Anki's Cozmo robot	https://www.digitaldreamlabs.com/pages/cozmo
Amazon's Alexa	https://developer.amazon.com/en-US/alexa
Cognimates AI platform	http://cognimates.me/home/
PlushPal	https://www.plushpal.app/
RoBoHoN	https://robohon.com/global/
PictoBlox	https://pictoblox.ai/

Fig. 5.2 Research
methods

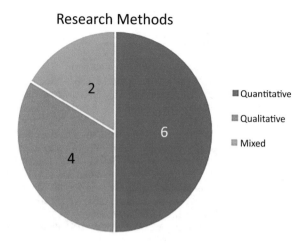

5.4 Conclusion

This chapter provides an overview of AI literary studies in ECE, focusing on research methods, pedagogical strategies, learning content, AI tools, and assessment methods. Although there were few studies on AI literacy for early childhood education, the existing references did provide new insights into various aspects of AI literacy for children. This chapter would provide valuable directions for AI education in early childhood education and serve as a reference for future AI literacy research in the digital society.

Researchers should design more interesting AI activities for children, such as interacting or playing with AI robots, which could change their existing attitudes toward AI. For example, Tazume et al. (2020) designed play with AI robots (i.e., RoBoHoN) activities for children. Results show that "children were strongly motivated to engage with human-type AI media" (Tazume et al., 2020, p. 328). Moreover, future researchers will develop quantitative and qualitative methods to evaluate children's learning outcome (i.e., knowledge, attitudes, and motivation) through pre and post-knowledge tests, surveys, questionnaires, and observations. Furthermore, future studies should explore what types of learning contents and teaching methods are more suitable for early childhood education and what kind of teacher training is necessary for kindergarteners. Lastly, most studies were conducted in developed countries/regions, such as the United States, Austria, Germany, Denmark, Sweden, Japan, Hong Kong, and Australia. Recommend that future research needs to investigate how AI literacy in early childhood can be applied in developing countries.

Table 5.4 Assessment methods

Studies	Details of assessments
Knowledge assessments/tests	
Williams (2018); Williams et al. (2019a, b)	Rule-based systems assessment: 1. Control: Which of these is rock? Rock, paper, or scissors? 2. We teach the robot the normal rules. Then, Sally plays rock and the robot plays paper, who does the robot think has won? Sally or the robot? 3. Sally plays paper five times. What does the robot think she will play next? Rock, paper, or scissors? 4. The robot thinks that Sally will play paper next. What will the robot play so that it can beat Sally? Rock, paper, or scissors? 5. We changed the rules so that they are all opposite rules (paper beats scissors). Sally plays scissors and the robot plays paper. Who does the robot think has won? Sally or the robot? Supervised machine learning: 1. Control: Which one of these foods is bad for your teeth? Strawberry, ice cream, or corn? 2. You start the robot and put strawberries and tomatoes into the good group. Which group will the robot think chocolate goes in? The good group or the bad group? 3. What food does the robot think is most like a tomato? Strawberry, banana, or milk? 4. You put ice cream in the good category and bananas in the bad category. What category will the robot put corn in? The good category or the bad category? Generative AI assessment 1. Control: Which one of these notes will make the robot's eyes go orange? Purple note, orange note, or green note? 2. Priya asks the robot to play back with the bars in the middle. Does the robot play the same song or a different song? 3. Priya asks the robot to play back with the bars to the right. Does the robot play the same song or a different song? 4. Does the robot's song have to have the same notes as the input?
Lin et al. (2020)	Zhorai assessment (machine learning) 1. Which sentences could you say to Zhorai to create the following mind map? (this assesses their understanding of how knowledge is represented.) 2. What could you tell Zhorai about monkeys so that it could correctly guess that monkeys live in rainforests? (this assesses their understanding of how Zhorai learns.) 3. The following histogram is what Zhorai thinks about where "toucan" lives. Based on the histogram, which ecosystem would Zhorai think a toucan lives in? (This assesses their understanding of how Zhorai makes a decision.) 4. Which ecosystems do snakes live in? Why might Zhorai have a difficult time classifying snakes into one ecosystem even if it knew everything there is to know about them? (This is an open-ended question for assessing mistakes Zhorai may make.) 5. Have you tried saying "Zhorai" to Zhorai? If not, ask the teacher if you can try. Does Zhorai recognize its own name? If not, why do you think it doesn't? Can you think of another name that Zhorai won't recognize? (This is an open-ended question on Zhorai's internal natural language processing.)

(continued)

Table 5.4 (continued)

Studies	Details of assessments
Robot-based assessment	
Williams (2018); Williams et al. (2019a)	Which view do you agree with more, or are you somewhere in the middle? Robots follow rules/robots do not follow rules. I am smarter than robots/robots are smarter than me. Robots are like toys/robots are like people. Robots cannot learn new things/robots can learn new things. Robots are like friends/robots are like adults. Druga et al. (2019) intelligence attribution, truthfulness attribution, perceived understanding
Druga et al. (2019)	Intelligence attribution, truthfulness attribution, perceived understanding
Video analysis	
Kandlhofer et al. (2016)	To assess students' joyfulness to explore the different units and understanding about the AI fundamental concepts (e.g., carrying out correct actions in the activities)
Druga et al. (2022a, b)	Children's body language and non-verbal interactions
Vartiainen et al. (2020)	Children's interaction with a Teachable Machine

References

Druga, S., & Ko, A. J. (2021, June). How do children's perceptions of machine intelligence change when training and coding smart programs?. In *Interaction design and children* (pp. 49–61).

Druga, S., Vu, S. T., Likhith, E., & Qiu, T. (2019). Inclusive AI literacy for kids around the world. *Proceedings of FabLearn, 2019*, 104–111.

Druga, S., Christoph, F. L., & Ko, A. J. (2022a, April). Family as a third space for AI literacies: How do children and parents learn about AI together?. In *CHI Conference on Human Factors in Computing Systems* (pp. 1–17).

Druga, S., Christoph, F. L., & Ko, A. J. (2022b, April). Family as a third space for AI literacies: How do children and parents learn about AI together?. In *CHI Conference on Human Factors in Computing Systems*. ACM publications. (pp. 1–17).

Dwivedi, U. (2021, June). Introducing children to machine learning through machine teaching. In *Interaction design and children*. ACM publications. (pp. 641–643).

Eguchi, A., Okada, H., & Muto, Y. (2021). Contextualizing AI education for K-12 students to enhance their learning of AI literacy through culturally responsive approaches. *KI-Künstliche Intelligenz, 35*(2), 153–161.

Kandlhofer, M., Steinbauer, G., Hirschmugl-Gaisch, S., & Huber, P. (2016, October). Artificial intelligence and computer science in education: From kindergarten to university. In *2016 IEEE Frontiers in Education Conference (FIE)* (pp. 1–9). IEEE.

Kewalramani, S., Kidman, G., & Palaiologou, I. (2021). Using artificial intelligence (AI)-interfaced robotic toys in early childhood settings: A case for children's inquiry literacy. *European Early Childhood Education Research Journal, 29*(5), 652–668.

Lin, P., Van Brummelen, J., Lukin, G., Williams, R., & Breazeal, C. (2020, April). Zhorai: Designing a conversational agent for children to explore machine learning concepts. In *Proceedings of the AAAI Conference on Artificial Intelligence, 34*(09), 13381–13388.

Moher, D., Liberati, A., Tetzlaff, J., Altman, D. G., Altman, D., Antes, G., et al. (2009). Preferred reporting items for systematic reviews and meta-analyses: The PRISMA statement (Chinese edition). *Journal of Chinese Integrative Medicine, 7*(9), 889–896.

Su, J., & Yang, W. (2022). Artificial intelligence in early childhood education: A scoping review. *Computers and Education: Artificial Intelligence, 3*, 100049.

Su, J., & Zhong, Y. (2022). Artificial intelligence (AI) in early childhood education: Curriculum design and future directions. *Computers and Education: Artificial Intelligence, 3*, 100072.

Su, J., Zhong, Y., & Ng, D. T. K. (2022). A meta-review of literature on educational approaches for teaching AI at the K-12 levels in the Asia-Pacific region. *Computers and Education: Artificial Intelligence*, 100065.

Tazume, H., Morita, T., & Hotta, H. (2020, June). Young children's literacy and cognition to interactive AI robots: A multifaceted study of potential enhancement to early childhood education. In *EdMedia+ innovate learning* (pp. 323–328). Association for the Advancement of Computing in Education (AACE).

Tseng, T., Murai, Y., Freed, N., Gelosi, D., Ta, T. D., & Kawahara, Y. (2021, June). PlushPal: Storytelling with interactive plush toys and machine learning. In *Interaction design and children* (pp. 236–245).

Vartiainen, H., Tedre, M., & Valtonen, T. (2020). Learning machine learning with very young children: Who is teaching whom? *International Journal of Child-Computer Interaction, 25*, 100182. https://doi.org/10.1016/j.ijcci.2020.100182

Williams, R. (2018). *PopBots: Leveraging social robots to aid preschool children's artificial intelligence education* (Doctoral dissertation, Massachusetts Institute of Technology).

Williams, R., Park, H. W., & Breazeal, C. (2019a, May). A is for artificial intelligence: The impact of artificial intelligence activities on young children's perceptions of robots. In *Proceedings of the 2019 CHI Conference on Human Factors in Computing Systems* (pp. 1–11).

Williams, R., Park, H. W., Oh, L., & Breazeal, C. (2019b, July). Popbots: Designing an artificial intelligence curriculum for early childhood education. In *Proceedings of the AAAI Conference on Artificial Intelligence, 33*(01), 9729–9736.

Yang, W. (2022). Artificial intelligence education for young children: Why, what, and how in curriculum design and implementation. *Computers and Education: Artificial Intelligence, 3*, 100061.

Chapter 6
AI Literacy Education in Primary Schools

Based on the literature review in Chap. 5, we learn that even children as young as 4 years old have already grown up with AI. In our rapidly transforming digital world, equipping young learners with AI knowledge and skills will help ensure their employability and learning potential in their future. Moreover, AI is already present in their everyday life such as video games, AI toys, virtual assistants, and smart devices (e.g., Google Assistant, robotics dogs, Alexa devices). Teaching AI was not possible in the past; however, with age-appropriate curriculum and tools, primary students can now know and understand the working principles behind AI, use AI for learning purposes, and apply their knowledge to create artifacts to solve authentic problems. As such, there is a need to investigate the pedagogy, learning content, tools, and assessment methods involved to develop young learners' AI literacy.

Primary schools have started AI literacy education to foster students' AI fundamentals, applications, and limitations. Nonetheless, the way how educators teach about AI remains largely unanswered due to the scarcity of research on what primary school students can learn about AI and what pedagogical strategies or learning tools are appropriate for teaching primary school students AI (Chai et al., 2021). Given the challenges in implementing AI education as an immediate result of a limited amount of literature in this field, there is an urgent need to address AI education in primary school settings. This chapter aims to fill the research gaps to evaluate, synthesize, and present literature under the current primary school education landscape. Four research questions (RQ) were formulated:

RQ1: What are the pedagogical strategies used in AI literacy studies at the primary level?
RQ2: What learning content is appropriate in AI literacy studies at the primary level?
RQ3: What learning tools have been used in AI literacy studies at the primary level?
RQ4: What assessment methods have been used in AI literacy studies at the primary level?

6.1 Method

In this chapter, electronic databases, namely, ACM Digital library, Google Scholar, IEEE, ProQuest Education Collection, Scopus, and Web of Science, were utilized for the literature search because of their reliability, as they all include a very high number of peer-reviewed journals and conferences. This paper focuses on AI education in primary school settings and uses the right term as a crucial part of the searching process (Talbott et al., 2018). In this study, the keywords selected were ("AI" OR "artificial intelligence" OR "artificial intelligence literacy" OR "deep learning" OR "machine learning" OR "neural network*" OR "natural language processing" OR "chatbot") AND ("primary school" OR "elementary school" OR "primary education" OR "elementary education" OR "primary school student" OR "elementary school student" OR "primary school pupil" OR "elementary school pupil") AND ("learning" OR "teaching" OR "pedagogy" OR "curriculum" OR "assessment" OR" challenges"). "Artificial intelligence" as a word or in combination with others such as "literacy" was also included in the search string. "Deep learning" OR "machine learning" OR "neural network" OR "natural language processing" OR "chatbot" were also used as part of the context for the search, because they constitute a subset of artificial intelligence. "Primary" or "elementary" is the context on which this paper focuses. "Learning" OR "teaching" OR "pedagogy" OR "curriculum" OR "assessment" as the context to which AI education is also applied.

To narrow down the scope of the article search, a protocol was employed in advance to document the exclusion and inclusion criteria. The following articles were removed according to the following exclusion criteria: (1) editorials, magazines, books, book chapters, and dissertations were excluded as they are not subjected to scholarly peer reviews and are not related to the research topic or abstract (n = 36,320); (2) duplicated articles (n = 209); (3) articles that solely focused on artificial intelligence technologies and were not related to AI literacy (n = 978); (4) articles whose focus was not related to AI learning, teaching, pedagogy, curriculum, or assessment (n = 34); and (5) student participants were not within the age range of 6–14 years old (n-5). On the other hand, the inclusion criteria were the following: (1) the work was written in English; (2) the paper was published in a peer-reviewed journal or conference; (3) student participants were within 6–14 years old or currently studying in primary schools; (4) teachers, schools, or any stakeholders involved in teaching or learning of AI; and (5) the work answered one or more of the terms related to the topics of the RQs. After applying all these criteria, there were 37 articles to be analyzed. The scoping review in Fig. 6.1 employs the Preferred Reporting Items for Systematic Reviews and Meta-Analyses (PRISMA) flow diagram (Moher et al., 2009). The article selection procedure included steps such as identification, screening, eligibility, data extractions, and data analysis.

To verify coding reliability, 12 articles were randomly selected, blinded/coded, and reviewed by two researchers. Any disagreements and differences in the comprehension of the coding system were resolved to ensure inter-rater reliability. The data were then examined and summarized using a coding scheme.

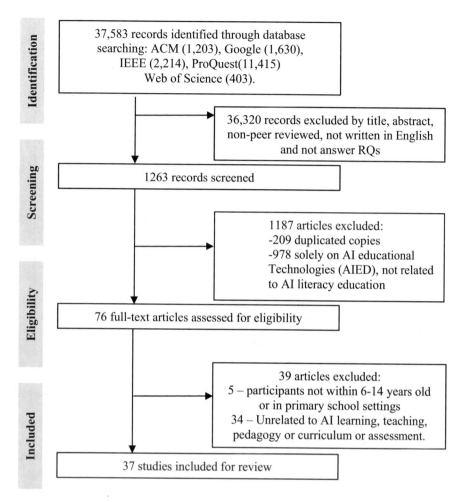

Fig. 6.1 PRISMA diagram

6.2 Results and Discussion

RQ1: What are the pedagogical strategies used in AI literacy studies?

The most often employed pedagogical strategies among the selected studies are project-based learning (11), play/game-based learning (11), and collaborative learning (8) (Table 6.1). First, project-based learning enables students to actively acquire a deeper knowledge through active exploration of real-world challenges and problems such as through teachable machine learning projects to understand the three steps of labeling, training and evaluation classifier (Melsion et al., 2021), and an assemble and programmable toy car to stimulate students' curiosity and motivation to learn about AI (Narahara & Kobayashi, 2018). Various levels of scratch projects

Table 6.1 Pedagogical approaches for AI literacy education in a primary school setting

Pedagogies	Descriptions	Sample studies	No
Project-based learning	Enables students to actively acquire a deeper knowledge through active exploration of real-world challenges and problems	Ali et al. (2019), Han et al. (2018), Heinze et al. (2010), Ho et al. (2019), Li and Song (2019), Narahara and Kobayashi (2018), Melsion et al. (2021), Ng et al. (2022), Rodríguez-García (2020, 2021), Vartiainen et al. (2020)	11
Game-based/ play-based learning	Refers to the borrowing of certain game principles or using play as a context for learning	Ali et al. (2019), Han et al. (2018), Heinze et al. (2010), Henry et al. (2021), Ho et al. (2019), Lee et al. (2020), Narahara and Kobayashi (2018), Ng et al. (2022), Shamir and Levin (2021, 2022), Voulgari et al. (2021)	11
Collaborative learning/ human-computer collaborative learning	Through peer instruction or human-machine interaction, students teach each other, address misunderstandings, clarify misconceptions, and discuss concepts to solve a problem, complete a task or create a product.	Ali et al. (2019), Eguchi et al. (2021), Heinze et al. (2010), Ho et al. (2019), Lee et al. (2020), Li and Song (2019), Tkáčová et al. (2020), Toivonen et al. (2020), Vartiainen et al. (2020)	8

are also used to teach AI according to the different age characteristics of students (Li & Song, 2019).

The second commonly mentioned method is game-based learning or playful learning approaches that refer to the borrowing of certain game principles or using play as a context for learning. This pedagogy is supported by various recent research. Henry et al. (2021) designed machine learning concepts in gameplay, and Voulgari et al. (2021) used ArtBot games to scaffold and introduce supervised learning, reinforcement learning, and AI algorithmic bias to students. In addition, Lee et al. (2020) created a collaborative game-based environment with a learning tool, PRIMARYAI, to enable upper primary school students to gain experience in image recognition, machine learning, planning, and automated decision-making.

Collaborative learning is also adopted to maximize students' learning outcomes. By allowing students to co-design (Toivonen et al., 2020), co-teach, and peer-teach the machine learning application (Vartiainen et al., 2020), these studies emphasize that learning is a collaborative process in which students effectively explore, engage in play, and apply knowledge (Ackermann, 2001).

When teaching AI to primary school students, several researchers use more than one pedagogical strategy. For example, building on the constructionist pedagogy of adopting a project-based approach, Ali et al. (2019) developed a hands-on collaborative Droodle Creativity game in his AI curriculum which involves designing new interfaces for students to explore AI. His study examines the project where students can think creatively and learn about AI by modeling the creative behavior of robots. The diversity of students between and within schools could be one explanation for the phenomena of this multiple use of pedagogical strategies (Chiu et al., 2021). Furthermore, other factors such as the primary school students' age, gender, background knowledge, educational surroundings, and available learning tools may have an impact on their learning styles and motivation to learn.

RQ2: What learning content is appropriate for primary school students in AI literacy studies?

Adapted from Bloom's taxonomy's cognitive levels (Bloom, 1956) and Ng et al. (2021)'s conceptual definition of AI learning inquiry, the learning content of AI education activities can be summarized in four categories which are (1) know and understand, (2) use and apply, (3) create and evaluate, and (4) AI ethics.

Know and Understand   The first cognitive level focuses on the AI foundations which are the basic AI foundations for every student who does not have prior AI or background and computer science knowledge. Researchers often design AI educational activities to engage students in acquiring authentic AI concepts, knowledge, and skills. Heinze et al. (2010) tailored AI activities in an age-appropriate and playful manner in order to effectively engage students to know and understand basic concepts, vocabulary, the history of science, and building blocks of AI. Furthermore, robotic exercises (Ho et al., 2019), frequent interactions with AI machines (Vartiainen et al., 2020), and greater AI exposure such as driving an AI toy car (Narahara & Kobayashi, 2018) demystify the AI concepts such as facial recognition and machine learning. These concepts can be explained to students in terms of computer algorithms that stimulate human-like behavior.

Use and Apply   The second cognitive level is allowing students to use and apply AI concepts and the related applications in various contexts. Lee et al. (2020) created engaging learning experiences that integrate artificial intelligence and life science for upper primary school students with game-based learning. A study conducted by Ho et al. (2019) asked six primary school students to turn a number-guessing robot into a self-learning lawn-bowling robot for a game of accuracy. Furthermore, the "PepperBot" social robot with AI multi-capabilities is already available in various Japanese schools. Eguchi et al. (2021) advocate including the PepperBot in the AI curriculum for primary school students to interact, gain hands-on experience, and program it while understanding the AI concepts and applying various AI functions.

Create and Evaluate   Aside from understanding AI concepts and applying AI through hands-on activities, a few researchers have extended AI literacy to the four cognitive levels to provide students opportunities to develop higher-order thinking and critical skills. There are various efforts underway to design and leverage various learning tools for AI artifact-making activities such as creating machine learning models; however, the learning outcomes of students are mixed. Google's Teachable Machine, for example, is a web-based tool that allows students to create machine learning models to recognize images and poses (Shamir & Levin, 2021, 2022). These two findings show that students are highly engaged in understanding machine learning concepts, whereas students also perceive self-efficacy in constructing and validating the neural network of an AI algorithm. Alternatively, in co-designing machine learning application workshops, Toivonen et al. (2020) invited 36 primary school participants to form groups of 4 or 5 to participate in a co-designing machine learning application workshop. The model resulted in sound recognition, while the prediction accuracy of students' work was low, and only one group fulfilled the required level of prediction accuracy. The results indicate that this machine learning content is suitable for students to develop their higher-order thinking skills, but there are practical pedagogical challenges in teaching AI learning content such as what tools to use, how to train, how long, and how much is enough for students to collect large enough and rich enough training data in order to solve the real-world problems of projects.

AI Ethics Many researchers include AI ethics in empirical studies as overused or poorly constructed AI could inflict irreparable harm on humans and society (Melsion et al. (2021). Heinze et al. (2010) discussed with Grade 5 and 6 students the two types of errors that humans and computers make. The notions that a science can be proven wrong in the context of hypotheses and a computer can also make mistakes and what this may signify are taught. For example, Melson et al. (2021) designed a bias visualization tool of machine learning integrated into an online educational platform (https://biaix.now.sh) which introduces not only the algorithmic bias among children concretely but also the notions of ethics and societal impact of AI. Students can become aware of AI ethics through discussing any concerns that arise from different AI applications (Han et al., 2018).

RQ3: What learning tools have been used in AI literacy studies?

This section identifies several age-appropriate learning tools under the current AI literacy primary schools landscape. An overview of these AI learning tools named in these selected studies is presented in Table 6.2.

Among these four categories, the introduction of intelligent agents (11) has become the most popular in primary school classrooms. The findings reveal that the main goal of suggesting intelligent agents is to teach machine learning concepts, a subset of AI concepts, which refer to a kind of data-driven thinking approach to execute real-time computation and make decisions. Intelligent agents such as Learning ML (Rodríguez-García et al., 2020, 2021; Voulgari et al., 2021) and Google Teachable Machine (Ali et al., 2019; Ng et al., 2022; Toivonen et al., 2020) are the appropriate learning tools to make such machine learning concepts understandable.

Other than intelligent agents that focus on data-driven AI techniques, many hardware, software, and unplugged activities are also targeted to scaffold AI concepts, such as the ethical aspects of AI. In terms of hardware-focused learning tools, robotics is commonly mentioned and seems to be promising in terms of supporting AI

Table 6.2 Learning tools in AI literacy primary school education

Type	No	Definitions	Learning tools	Studies
Hardware-focused	8	Use physical artifacts in AI literacy studies such as robots, small single-board computers or microcontroller devices	ArtBot, Jibo, and PopBots; Zumi robot; Micro:Bit; HuskyLens by DFRobot; Pepper robot by SoftBank robotics; Lego Mindstorm; Lawn-bowling robot; Raspberry Pi	Ali et al. (2019), Eguchi et al. (2021), Heinze et al. (2010), Ho et al. (2019), Lin et al. (2021), Narahara and Kobayashi (2018), Ng et al. (2021), Voulgari et al. (2021)
Software or open source-focused	10	Use digital artifacts or open-source platforms in AI literacy studies such as programming language, neural networks, machine learning software toolkits	Web application (HTML + JavaScript); AI Chatbot, Scratch, Snap!, App Inventor Grad-CAM; Python and Tensorflow; Quick Draw, image stylizer, gamified Kahoot game; Thing Translator; Watson Speech to Text; Watson Visual Recognition; Watson Natural Language Understanding; Google Maps, Google Drawings, and Google Trends; Connect the Dots; ITMS software, virtual simulation of teaching platform, SmartVoice	Han et al. (2018), Mariescu-Istodor and Jormanainen (2019), Marques et al. (2020), Melsion et al. (2021), Narahara and Kobayashi (2018), Ng et al. (2022), Shamir and Levin (2021), Tkáčová et al. (2020), Toivonen et al. (2020), Wei et al. (2020)
Intelligent agents	11	Intelligent agents to teach AI by performing real-time computation based on the inputs to make decisions such as machine learning trainers, chatbots to build machine learning models without coding	Google Teachable Machine; Droodle Creativity; AI-in-a-Box; Squirrel AI; Primary AI; Scratch; code.org; LearningML platform (https://learningml.org.)	Ali et al. (2019), Gong et al. (2020), Lee et al. (2020), Li and Song (2019), Ng et al. (2021, 2022), Rodríguez-García (2020, 2021), Shamir and Levin (2021), Toivonen et al. (2020), Voulgari et al. (2021)
Unplugged	8	Unplugged activities to teach AI studies without a computer, such as role-playing and storytelling	Abstract drawing; paper prototyping activity; writing story with robots; role-playing games; YouTube learning video; hand-drawing illustration; unplugged activities (csunplugged.org); digital story creation	Ali et al. (2019), Heinze et al. (2010), Henry et al. (2021), Ho et al. (2019), Mariescu-Istodor and Jormanainen (2019), Lucas (2012), Ng et al. (2021, 2022)

education. Jibo, PopBots (Ali et al., 2019), and lawn-bowling robots (Ho et al., 2019) motivate and engage students in AI learning through games and competition. On the other hand, software-focused learning tools such as Grad-Cam (Melsion et al., 2021), Quick Draw and image stylizer (Ng et al., 2022; Tkáčová et al., 2020), and AI Chatbots (Shamir & Levin, 2021) provide a convenient way to access, visualize, and produce basic AI learning content.

In addition, Shamir and Levin (2021) designed an AI curriculum for Israeli students to engage in conversations with AI Chatbot in order to understand the Turing test concept. Alternatively, a few researchers have offered unplugged activities to foster their conceptual understanding of AI such as abstract drawing, hand-drawing illustration (Ali et al., 2019; Mariescu-Istodor & Jormanainen, 2019), and writing stories with robots (Heinze et al., 2010; Ng et al. (2022).

RQ4: What assessment methods have been used in AI literacy studies?

As shown in Table 6.3, qualitative (n = 12), mixed methods (n = 7), and quantitative (n = 5) are used in AI literacy empirical studies for data collection. It is noted that the discussion paper and review papers are excluded in this section.

Qualitative evidence is collected through assessing students' artifacts, role-play performance, games and competition, interviews, and video recordings to examine students' motivation and engagement in learning AI as well as evaluate the suitability of the teaching methods in primary school students' classrooms. For example, Lee et al. (2020) revealed that the test run driving a toy car on a miniature track which involves students assembling, training, and testing the AI model can stimulate students' curiosity to learn about AI. Others use the activity of role-play games, students' artifact for a lawn-bowling robot competition, and music gamification competition to arouse students' motivation, enhance their engagement, and cultivate their basic AI literacy and computational thinking (Henry et al., 2021; Han et al. 2018; Ho et al. (2019). Vartiainen and Valtonen's (2020) study focuses on evaluating the content and teaching method through interviews and video recordings to observe, explore, and explain the human-computer relationship when students interact with a teachable machine. The result shows that students have "fun" and a "nice"

Table 6.3 Assessment methods

Assessment methods	No (37)	Studies
Qualitative	12	Dai et al. (2020), Han et al. (2018), Heinze et al. (2010), Henry et al. (2021), Ho et al. (2019), Mariescu-Istodor and Jormanainen (2019), Lee et al. (2020), Li and Song (2019), Lucas (2009), Ottenbreit-Leftwich et al. (2021), Toivonen et al. (2020), Vartiainen and Valtonen (2020)
Quantitative	5	Chai et al. (2020a, b, 2021), Lin et al. (2021), Rodríguez-Garciá et al. (2021)
Mixed method	7	Ali et al. (2019), Gong et al. (2020), Melsion et al. (2021), Ng et al. (2022), Shamir and Levin (2021, 2022), Voulgari et al. (2021)
Discussion papers	7	Eguchi et al. (2021), Narahara and Kobayashi (2018), Rodríguez-García (2020), Steinbauer et al. (2021), Tkáčová et al. (2020), Touretzky et al. (2019), Wei et al. (2020)
Review articles	6	Marques et al. (2020), Ng et al. (2021), Sanusi and Oyelere (2020), Su et al. (2022), Tedre et al. (2021), Yang (2019)

learning experience which suggests that a teachable machine fosters the intellectual curiosity of students to learn about AI (Vartiainen et al., 2020).

On the contrary, quantitative methods collect data through surveys and questionnaires to examine the learning outcomes of students and their perception of AI education. For example, online pre- and post-questionnaires are designed for students to evaluate their understanding of the concept of the machine learning metric and data training (Rodríguez-Garciá et al., 2021). Others use surveys to examine students' perception of their behavioral intention, motivation, readiness, relevance, and anxiety regarding AI education (Chai et al., 2020a, b, 2021) and the effectiveness of the motivational model design in the context of AI learning in primary schools (Lin et al., 2021).

Also, seven studies used mixed methods to collect data from multiple sources including focus groups, questionnaire surveys, field visits, interviews, and artifact assessments (Gong et al., 2020; Shamir & Levin, 2021; Voulgari et al., 2021).

Overall, artifact-based assessment, interviews, surveys, and questionnaires are often used in data collection procedures, whereas games and competition have been increased in the research design method recently. Apart from the Torrance test (Ali et al., 2019), pre- and post-assessment of gender bias assessment (Melsion et al., 2021) and online knowledge assessment (Rodríguez-Garciá et al., 2021) for evaluating students' learning outcomes, many studies use subjective measures such as self-reported surveys or artifact assessment. These studies reveal the inadequacy of rubric-based, evaluative mechanisms to assess the quality of suggested methodologies.

6.3   Conclusions

This paper presents a systematic review mapping process and offers an exploratory perspective on AI education in today's primary school setting. The learning content described in the reviewed articles was grouped into four categories of know and understand, use and apply, create and evaluate, and AI ethics. Surveys and questionnaires, artifact-based assessment, and interviews are often used in data collection for assessment purposes. This study, in addition to shedding light on the learning content and assessment methodologies of AI education in primary education, also reveals the most commonly used pedagogical approaches as being project-based, play/game-based, and collaborative/human-computer interactive teaching strategies that will be suitable in primary school contexts. It illuminates that many researchers use a combination of different pedagogical approaches and that the taught content may change to meet the diverse requirements and cognitive skills of students and collection procedure, whereas games and competition have been used in research methods recently.

Although this review contributes to offering an exploratory perspective on AI education in today's primary school setting, one limitation lies in the scarcity of available literature. AI literacy learning and teaching in primary school settings, however, appear to be in its infancy. Future directions can be focused on this to enrich the field of AI literacy in primary education. To advocate AI literacy education for all, priority should be placed on developing an AI curriculum that includes primary school students to guide educators to have lesson designs with age-appropriate pedagogies, learning tools, and assessment methodologies. Moreover, the implementation of AI education also requires more professional development for pre-service and in-service primary school teachers. For the purpose of developing AI educational initiatives, curriculum materials, and pedagogies that are applicable to a wide range and diversity of educators and primary school students, further studies on the teachers' perspectives, instructional practices, and effectiveness of pedagogical strategies on AI education are also of high relevance to promote AI education in the primary schools landscape. We hope that this review will inspire researchers, educators, and the government to begin the discussion on what to teach and how to teach, implement, and evaluate AI literacy education for primary school students in the future. In fact, countries have started their AI curricula in primary school settings that are designed by researchers and collaborators and endorsed by the government. Educators should start by helping students solidify their cognitive development about technological knowledge and skill acquisition, learning, and innovation skills. Students should identify AI's societal impacts in their everyday life. Moreover, we develop children's learning about how technology works through powerful metaphors, playful experience, and simulations in the form of hands-on experiential activities. Finally, we work with students to develop their understanding of how design choices impact others so that children can design their own intelligent robot solutions to various problems.

References

Ackermann, E. (2001). Piaget's constructivism, Papert's constructionism: What's the difference? *Future of Learning Group Publication, 5*(3), 438.

Ali, S., Payne, B. H., Williams, R., Park, H. W., & Breazeal, C. (2019). Constructionism, ethics, and creativity: Developing primary and middle school artificial intelligence education. In *International workshop on education in artificial intelligence k-12 (eduai'19)* (pp. 1–4).

Bloom, B. S. (1956). Taxonomy of educational objectives: The classification of educational goals. *Cognitive domain.*

Chai, C. S., Lin, P. Y., Jong, M. S. Y., Dai, Y., Chiu, T. K., & Huang, B. (2020a, August). Factors influencing students' behavioral intention to continue artificial intelligence learning. In *2020 International Symposium on Educational Technology (ISET)* (pp.147–150). IEEE.

Chai, C., Lin, P., Jong, M., Dai, Y., & Chiu, T. (2020b). Primary students' readiness for learning of artificial intelligence: A case study in Beijing. In *Proceedings of the 28th international conference on computers in education.* Asia-pacific Society for Computers in education.

Chai, C. S., Lin, P. Y., Jong, M. S. Y., Dai, Y., Chiu, T. K., & Qin, J. (2021). Perceptions of and behavioral intentions towards learning artificial intelligence in primary school students. *Educational Technology & Society, 24*(3), 89–101.

Chiu, T. K., Meng, H., Chai, C. S., King, I., Wong, S., & Yam, Y. (2021). Creation and evaluation of a pretertiary artificial intelligence (AI) curriculum. *IEEE Transactions on Education., 65*, 30–39.

Dai, Y., Chai, C. S., Lin, P. Y., Jong, M. S. Y., Guo, Y., & Qin, J. (2020). Promoting students' well-being by developing their readiness for the artificial intelligence age. *Sustainability, 12*(16), 6597.

Eguchi, A., Okada, H., & Muto, Y. (2021). Contextualizing AI education for K-12 students to enhance their learning of AI literacy through culturally responsive approaches. *KI-Künstliche Intelligenz, 35*(2), 153–161.

Gong, X., Tang, Y., Liu, X., Jing, S., Cui, W., Liang, J., & Wang, F. Y. (2020, October). K-9 artificial intelligence education in Qingdao: Issues, challenges and suggestions. In *2020 IEEE International Conference on Networking, Sensing and Control (ICNSC)* (pp. 1–6). IEEE.

Han, X., Hu, F., Xiong, G., Liu, X., Gong, X., Niu, X., ... & Wang, X. (2018). Design of AI+ curriculum for primary and secondary schools in Qingdao. In *2018 Chinese Automation Congress (CAC)* (pp. 4135–4140). IEEE.

Heinze, C. A., Haase, J., & Higgins, H. (2010). An action research report from a multi-year approach to teaching artificial intelligence at the k-6 level. In *First AAAI symposium on educational advances in artificial intelligence.*

Henry, J., Hernalesteen, A., & Collard, A. S. (2021). Teaching artificial intelligence to K-12 through a role-playing game questioning the intelligence concept. *KI-Künstliche Intelligenz, 35*(2), 171–179.

Ho, J. W., Scadding, M., Kong, S. C., Andone, D., Biswas, G., Hoppe, H. U., & Hsu, T. C. (2019). Classroom activities for teaching artificial intelligence to primary school students. In *Proceedings of international conference on computational thinking education* (pp. 157–159).

Lee, S., Mott, B., Ottenbriet-Leftwich, A., Scribner, A., Taylor, S., Glazewski, K., ... & Lester, J. (2020, June). Designing a collaborative game-based learning environment for ai-infused inquiry learning in elementary school classrooms. In *Proceedings of the 2020 ACM conference on innovation and technology in computer science education* (pp. 566–566).

Li, K., & Song, S. (2019, June). Application of artificial intelligence in primary and secondary schools: A case study of scratch. In *International conference on applications and techniques in cyber security and intelligence* (pp. 2026–2030). Springer

Lin, P. Y., Chai, C. S., Jong, M. S. Y., Dai, Y., Guo, Y., & Qin, J. (2021). Modeling the structural relationship among primary students' motivation to learn artificial intelligence. *Computers and Education: Artificial Intelligence, 2*, 100006.

Lucas, J. M. (2009). K-6 outreach using "computer science unplugged". *Journal of Computing Sciences in Colleges, 24*(6), 62–63.

Mariescu-Istodor, R., & Jormanainen, I. (2019, November). Machine learning for high school students. In *Proceedings of the 19th Koli calling international conference on computing education research* (pp. 1–9).

Marques, L. S., Gresse von Wangenheim, C., & Hauck, J. C. (2020). Teaching machine learning in school: A systematic mapping of the state of the art. *Informatics in Education, 19*(2), 283–321.

Melsión, G. I., Torre, I., Vidal, E., & Leite, I. (2021, June). Using explainability to help children understand gender bias in AI. In *Interaction design and children* (pp. 87–99).

Moher, D., Liberati, A., Tetzlaff, J., Altman, D. G., & PRISMA Group*. (2009). Preferred reporting items for systematic reviews and meta-analyses: The PRISMA statement. *Annals of Internal Medicine, 151*(4), 264–269.

Narahara, T., & Kobayashi, Y. (2018). Personalizing homemade bots with plug & play AI for STEAM education. In *SIGGRAPH Asia 2018 technical briefs* (pp. 1–4).

Ng, D. T. K., Leung, J. K. L., Chu, S. K. W., & Qiao, M. S. (2021). Conceptualizing AI literacy: An exploratory review. *Computers and Education: Artificial Intelligence, 2*, 100041.

Ng, D. T. K., Luo, W. Y., Chan, H. M. Y., & Chu, S. K. W. (2022). An examination on primary students' development in AI literacy through digital story writing. *Computers & Education: Artificial Intelligence*, 100054.

Ottenbreit-Leftwich, A., Glazewski, K., Jeon, M., Hmelo-Silver, C., Mott, B., Lee, S., & Lester, J. (2021, March). How do elementary students conceptualize artificial intelligence?

In *Proceedings of the 52nd ACM technical symposium on computer science education* (pp. 1261–1261).

Rodríguez-García, J. D., Moreno-León, J., Román-González, M., & Robles, G. (2020, October). Introducing artificial intelligence fundamentals with LearningML: Artificial intelligence made easy. In *Eighth international conference on technological ecosystems for enhancing multiculturality* (pp. 18–20).

Rodríguez-García, J. D., Moreno-León, J., Román-González, M., & Robles, G. (2021, March). Evaluation of an online intervention to teach artificial intelligence with LearningML to 10-16-year-old students. In *Proceedings of the 52nd ACM technical symposium on computer science education* (pp. 177–183).

Sanusi, I. T., & Oyelere, S. S. (2020, October). Pedagogies of machine learning in K-12 context. In *2020 IEEE Frontiers in Education Conference (FIE)* (pp. 1–8). IEEE.

Shamir, G., & Levin, I. (2021). Neural network construction practices in elementary school. *KI-Künstliche Intelligenz, 35*(2), 181–189.

Shamir, G., & Levin, I. (2022). Teaching machine learning in elementary school. *International Journal of Child-Computer Interaction, 31*, 100415.

Steinbauer, G., Kandlhofer, M., Chklovski, T., Heintz, F., & Koenig, S. (2021). A differentiated discussion about AI education K-12. *KI-Künstliche Intelligenz, 35*(2), 131–137.

Su, J., Zhong, Y., & Ng, D. T. K. (2022). A meta-review of literature on educational approaches for teaching AI at the K-12 levels in the Asia-Pacific region. *Computers and Education: Artificial Intelligence*, 100065.

Talbott, E., Maggin, D. M., Van Acker, E. Y., & Kumm, S. (2018). Quality indicators for reviews of research in special education. *Exceptionality, 26*(4), 245–265.

Tedre, M., Toivonen, T., Kahila, J., Vartiainen, H., Valtonen, T., Jormanainen, I., & Pears, A. (2021). Teaching machine learning in K–12 classroom. In *Pedagogical and technological trajectories for artificial intelligence education.* IEEE Access, 9, 110558-110572.

Tkáčová, Z., Šnajder, L. U., & Guniš, J. (2020, October). Artificial intelligence–a new topic in computer science curriculum at primary and secondary schools: Challenges, opportunities, tools and approaches. In *2020 43rd International Convention on Information, Communication and Electronic Technology (MIPRO)* (pp. 747–749). IEEE.

Toivonen, T., Jormanainen, I., Kahila, J., Tedre, M., Valtonen, T., & Vartiainen, H. (2020, July). Co-designing machine learning apps in K–12 with primary school children. In *2020 IEEE 20th International Conference on Advanced Learning Technologies (ICALT)* (pp. 308–310). IEEE.

Touretzky, D., Martin, F., Seehorn, D., Breazeal, C., & Posner, T. (2019, February). Special session: AI for K-12 guidelines initiative. In *Proceedings of the 50th ACM technical symposium on computer science education* (pp. 492–493).

Vartiainen, H., Tedre, M., & Valtonen, T. (2020). Learning machine learning with very young children: Who is teaching whom? *International Journal of Child-Computer Interaction, 25*, 100182.

Voulgari, I., Zammit, M., Stouraitis, E., Liapis, A., & Yannakakis, G. (2021, June). Learn to machine learn: Designing a game based approach for teaching machine learning to primary and secondary education students. In *Interaction design and children* (pp. 593–598).

Wei, Q., Li, M., Xiang, K., & Qiu, X. (2020, August). Analysis and strategies of the professional development of information technology teachers under the vision of artificial intelligence. In *2020 15th International Conference on Computer Science & Education (ICCSE)* (pp. 716–721). IEEE.

Yang, X. (2019). Accelerated move for AI education in China. *ECNU Review of Education, 2*(3), 347–352.

Chapter 7
AI Literacy Education in Secondary Schools

As AI literacy has grown its popularity across countries and regions around the world to design and implement AI curricula in secondary school levels. According to the report of UNESCO (2022), 11 member states have designed, endorsed, and implemented AI government-endorsed curricula. In the review of Ng et al. (2021b), over 14 countries around the world (including the United States, China, Spain, Hong Kong, Finland, Brazil, and Germany) have begun to promote secondary students' AI competences and equip them with related knowledge, skills, and attitudes.

Based on the literature review in the previous chapters, we can find that the learning content, pedagogy, and tools of AI literacy education are still continuing to develop to best foster students' AI literacy. This chapter provides an overview of how AI literacy is developed at junior and secondary levels. After illustrating the research method including literature search and data analysis, this chapter reviews the pedagogy, content, tools, and assessment methods used in the selected studies. We analyzed the current state of AI literacy education and suggested future directions regarding how to best teach and learn AI in secondary levels. Four research questions (RQ) formed the basis of this review:

RQ1: What are the pedagogical strategies used at the secondary level?
RQ2: What learning contents are appropriate for students at their junior and senior secondary level?
RQ3: What are the learning tools used at the secondary level?
RQ4: What are the assessment methods used at the secondary level?

7.1 Method

To ensure that the search encompassed all of the evidence-based SSCI literature, the researchers used two trusted citation index databases, Web of Science and Scopus. First, we searched the two databases for publications published between 2016 and 2022 using the phrase ("AI" OR "artificial intelligence" OR " artificial intelligence literacy" OR "deep learning" OR "machine learning" OR "neural network*" OR "natural language processing" OR "chatbot") AND ("secondary school" OR "middle school" OR "secondary education" OR "pre-tertiary education" OR "secondary student" OR "middle school student" OR "pre-tertiary student") AND ("learning" OR "teaching" OR "pedagogy" OR "curriculum") in either the title, the abstract, main text, or keywords were downloaded and reviewed by the researchers. As of 3 March 2022, this gave us a total of 307 articles in the 2 databases.

Then, two experienced researchers decided if they were appropriate for the goal of this study. During this search, a set of inclusion and exclusion criteria were established to avoid biases in the articles selection. To begin, all of the studies that were chosen had to be journal articles, discussion papers, case studies, or conference papers from the aforementioned databases. Second, the studies have to be relevant to AI literacy and teaching/learning AI concepts in the field of education (e.g., artificial intelligence, machine learning, deep learning, natural language, neural networks, chatbots). Sun's article, for example, was excluded because it used 5G and AI technologies in English instruction instead of teaching AI concepts. However, because of a lack of peer review, editorials and novels are not included. Following the exclusion of irrelevant studies, a total of 38 articles were discovered. An overview of the search protocol in a PRISMA diagram is presented in Fig. 7.1.

The selected papers were qualitatively categorized using the constant comparative method espoused by Glaser (1965). We examined the major content of the articles and identified related meaningful concepts for thematic analysis. To verify coding reliability, all of the papers were reviewed by two researchers who resolved conflicts by discussing the disputed studies in order to ensure inter-rater reliability. The data were then examined and summarized using a coding scheme. The scheme was modified from Ng's (2021a, b) scheme, which includes pedagogical approaches, technologies/tools used, learning material, and learning outcomes.

7.2 Results and Discussion

RQ1: What are the pedagogical strategies used in AI literacy studies?

As indicated in Table 7.1, this section outlines the three major pedagogical methods and strategies used in the studies: project-/problem-based learning (24), collaborative learning (23), and experiential learning (15).

First, project-/problem-based learning is the most often used pedagogy to foster students' AI literacy. For example, Vachovsky et al. (2016) involved 24 girls in

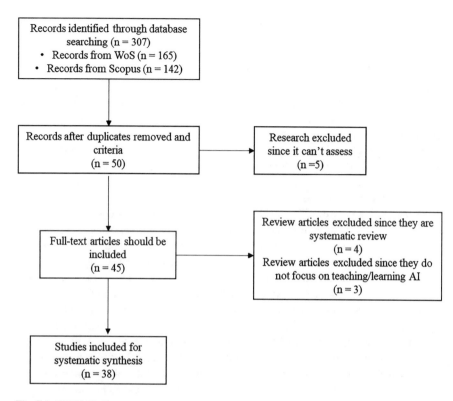

Fig. 7.1 PRISMA diagram

Table 7.1 Pedagogical approaches for AI literacy education

Pedagogies	Descriptions	Sample studies	N	Percent (%)
Project-/ problem-based learning	Learning approaches to engage students to gain knowledge and skills by working to investigate authentic questions, problems, or challenges	Rodríguez-García (2020), Sakulkueakulsuk et al. (2018), Wan et al. (2020)	24	63.2
Collaborative learning	This pedagogy allows students to learn how to communicate and work with classmates to gain AI knowledge and manipulate with smart devices	Deng et al. (2021), Gao and Wang (2019), Gong et al. (2018)	23	60.5
Experiential learning	Process of learning by doing through hands-on experiences and reflection; students could gain better understanding to connect theories and knowledge learned in the classroom to real-world situations	Chiu et al. (2021), Morris (2020), Tamborg et al. (2022)	15	39.5

authentic projects to learn computer vision, robotics, and natural language processing in a summer camp. According to the survey, 95.8% of students believe that the projects they built can benefit society. Furthermore, students said the course was interesting (83.3%) and increased their confidence in using AI (75%). Rodrguez-Garca et al. (2020) presented the LearningML projects (a low-floor high-ceiling platform to learn machine learning by doing) to provide the principles of machine learning to students in order for them to acquire knowledge and become critical thinking citizens. We can observe that project-/problem-based learning gives authentic settings such as constructing models of athletic moves (Zimmermann-Niefield et al., 2019) and meaningful scientific and STEM contexts that could motivate them to learn AI through a sense of authenticity and real-world applicability (Sakulkueakulsuk et al., 2018; Wan et al., 2020).

Collaborative learning allows students to learn how to communicate and collaborate with classmates to gain AI knowledge and manipulate with smart devices (e.g., Deng et al., 2021; Gao & Wang, 2019; Gong et al., 2018). Gong et al. (2018), for example, engaged students to various positions such as project managers, software designers, hardware designers, and art designers in order to build smart vehicles in authentic settings. Another study, done by Gao and Wang (2019), invited students to act as buyers and sellers in order to identify problems and shortcomings about intelligent functions in smart home systems. Kaspersen (2021) assigned three to four students in a group to design ML models that predict if a person will vote for a particular political party. A combination of collaborative learning and project-/problem-based learning could significantly improve students' higher-order thinking skills, such as problem-solving, leadership, project management, and creativity (e.g., Deng et al., 2021; Gong et al., 2018).

The third common method is to engage students in playful and experiential learning by using Teachable Machine (Chiu et al., 2021; Tamborg et al., 2022), Code.org games (Ng & Chu, 2021), intelligent agents, chatbots, Cognimates (Gong et al., 2018), and syntax-based programs (e.g., Python) (Gong et al., 2018; Gunasilan, 2021) (Estevez et al., 2019; Kahn et al., 2018). These activities give students hands-on experience investigating what AI is, visualizing complex ideas (Reyes et al., 2020), and developing building ML models (Sakulkueakulsuk et al., 2018). Although these activities provide students with hands-on experience to scaffold AI, most studies further applied minds-on collaborative projects to encourage students to further build knowledge by creating digital and tangible artifacts in constructionist ways. In this way, educators could help students achieve higher cognition levels and apply AI skills and knowledge to address real-world problems for future learning and career challenges (Chai et al., 2020).

RQ2: What learning tools have been used in AI literacy studies?

As technology advances, more age-appropriate learning artifacts enable students to visualize the operations of complex concepts that were previously impossible. Aligned with Sanusi et al. (2021) and Ng et al. (2021a, b), four major categories of resources and technologies have been identified: conversational agents,

Table 7.2 Learning artifacts

	Definition	Learning artifacts examples	Sample studies
Hardware-focused artifacts	Use physical artifacts to learn AI such as robotics, sensors and Arduino devices	CUHKiCar, educational robot, drones, VR devices Alpha dog robot, Raspberry Pi Raspbian, four-wheel drive chassis, Micro:Bits	Chai et al. (2020), Chiu et al. (2021), Tamborg et al. (2022)
Software-focused artifacts	Use digital artifacts to learn AI such as block/syntax-based programming and simulation	Prolog, image stylizer, Colab (Python programming), Jupyter notebooks, Blockly, WebAPPs, cognitive services, Google Collaborator, Scratch, Snap!, MIT STEP Lab, game design	Chiu et al. (2021), Norouzi et al. (2020), Gunasilan (2021)
Intelligent agents	Use intelligent agents such as expert systems, machine learning trainers, chatbots to build their custom machine learning models without coding	Scratch, Google's Teachable Machine, LearningML platform, ecraft2learn, Machine Learning for Kids, Cognimates, Code.org AI Ocean, Face AI Scratch, Machine Learning for kids, AI model trainer, ecraft2learn, SmileyCluster, chatbots	Rodríguez-García (2020), Sabuncuoglu (2020), Wan et al. (2020)
Unplugged	Use learning activities to learn AI without a computer such as lecture, case study, role-playing, and storytelling	Lectures, career talk, textbook, case study, webinar, role-playing, storytelling, debating	Gunasilan (2021), Deng et al. (2021), Gong et al. (2018)

programming environments, robotics, and unplugged activity. Table 7.2 is a list of examples of how to use AI learning artifacts to learn AI.

First, hardware- and software-focused artifacts engaged students in making and creating AI-driven applications using physical and digital artifacts. Chiu et al. (2021), for example, constructed a robotic car named CUHKiCar with built-in AI functions to provide interactive learning experiences for students doing face-tracking and line-following tasks. It was discovered that students improved significantly in perceived knowledge gain, confidence, motivation, and AI readiness. Chai et al. (2020) conducted a study in which students could use Alpha dog robots and design algorithms to recognize physical characteristics such as temperature, voice, face, and images. It helps students to build AI solutions using AI and mathematics knowledge (e.g., calculus and statistics).

Second, it has been determined that most of the hardware and software should be manipulated with built-in and add-on AI-driven features that enable students to build machine learning intelligent agents and machine learning models without the need for programming (Chiu et al., 2021; Kaspersen et al., 2021). This provides students with opportunities to lower the learning barrier and gain access to more advanced concepts that were previously impossible. In our selected studies, most of them focused on tool-based learning to provide students with hands-on experiences to learn the fundamental AI/computer science knowledge, skills, and concepts. The tools allow students to visualize the complex knowledge and encourage them to collect between AI applications and the underlying knowledge. Chatbots (Rodrguez-Garca et al., 2020), Scratch, and Teachable Machine (Tamborg et al., 2022), for example, inspire students to solve authentic problems using these tools. Students can learn the functional and critical parts of using AI-driven technologies through tool-based AI learning. In addition to learning technical knowledge and skills (e.g., computer vision, virtual reality, art design) (Gong et al., 2018), students' critical thinking skills are required to express and apply knowledge, as well as communicate and interact with the tools to solve authentic problems (Kaspersen et al., 2021).

RQ3: What learning contents are appropriate for junior and senior secondary students in AI literacy studies?

This section provides a summary of the learning content that secondary students need to master at the junior (14) and senior (22) levels (see Table 7.3). Educators need to understand the cognitive development of each step of AI learning in order to design developmentally appropriate instruction. Prior research has shown that junior secondary students should focus on preliminary and simple AI concepts such as machine learning, natural language processing, and Turing tests in the junior AI curriculum (Chiu et al., 2021; Fernández-Martnez et al., 2021; Ng & Chu, 2021). Educators should design hands-on experiential learning for students to taste and use related AI applications, as well as explore their benefits, challenges, ethical concerns, and shortcomings (Sabuncuoglu, 2020; Wan et al., 2020). In this manner,

Table 7.3 Learning contents in junior and secondary school levels

Levels	Learning contents samples	Sample studies
Junior level	**Experiencing AI:** Using AI applications, benefits, and disadvantages of using AI, machine learning, face recognition, image stylizer, machine generation of creative content, experimentation of using AI technologies **Simple AI concepts:** History/introduction/recent development of AI and its subareas, differences between humans and machines, natural language processing, scratch activities on machine learning and image recognition, machine learning **Societal impacts and AI ethics:** AI ethics, societal impacts of AI, machine reasoning, problem-solving	Chiu et al. (2021), Fernández-Martínez et al. (2021), Ng and Chu (2021)
Senior level	**Complex AI topics:** Natural language processing, computer vision, cognition, biomedical informatics, robotics, information networks, human-robot interactions, computational sustainability **AI technical components:** Fisher's exact test, inductive reasoning, nearest neighbor algorithm, correlation, graph search algorithms, computational game theory, optimization, agent-based modeling, probabilistic reasoning **AI literacy:** Understanding how ML works, the process behind creating ML models, and the ability to reflect on its personal and societal implications	Kaspersen et al. (2021), Kahn et al. (2018), Zhang and Du (2008)

students needed to apply these knowledge and skills to solve problems using well-defined hardware, software, and intelligent agents.

Senior secondary students could achieve greater cognition levels to develop technical algorithms and components (e.g., Fisher's exact test, inductive reasoning, nearest neighbor algorithm, correlation, graph search) (Vachovsky et al., 2016). They could experiment with more complex concepts like computational game theory, agent-based modeling, probabilistic reasoning, and graph theories (e.g., Estevez et al., 2019; Reyes et al., 2020). Students at both levels could create AI-driven solutions and models after knowing and understanding the AI knowledge, concerts, and skills process. Furthermore, students at both the junior and senior levels were required to explore the humanistic, sociological, and ethical implications of technology (Kaspersen et al., 2021). Additionally, students at all levels need to learn important competences (e.g., critical thinking, communication, collaboration, and creativity) in twenty-first century skills that will enable them to succeed in school and in their future workplace (e.g., Fernández-Martnez et al., 2021).

In general, our findings are consistent with Touretzky et al. (2019)'s five "major ideas" of AI, which state that students may learn how to utilize AI/computers to perceive the world using sensors, design with AI agents to maintain representation, reasoning, and learning from data. They were urged to apply intelligent agents to interact with humans in a natural way. Finally, students could learn how AI can have an impact on our digital society in both beneficial and detrimental ways. The categorization is also consistent with Ng's three dimensions of AI knowledge: AI concepts, practices, and perspectives (2021a, b). Using a sound cognition framework to foster AI literacy, educators should select appropriate levels of knowledge, concepts, and skills to meet the students' learning needs and development.

RQ4: What assessment methods have been used in AI literacy studies?

Researchers employed quantitative (14) and qualitative (27) assessments to investigate how children enhance their AI literacy skills (see Table 7.4). In this RQ, we double-classified "mixed-method research" into quantitative and qualitative evaluations, but the discussion papers were not coded.

Quantitative Methods Surveys and questionnaires were designed to assess students' knowledge acquisition via knowledge tests (e.g., Why do you think large amounts of data might matter?) and students' perceived abilities in order to better understand secondary students' AI literacy development (e.g., I have general knowledge about how AI is used today.) Zimmermann-Niefield et al., 2019; Chiu et al., 2021). Chiu et al. (2021) designed a questionnaire to understand students' intrinsic motivation, AI readiness, perceived abilities, and confidence. Chai et al. (2020) designed a 41-item questionnaire to assess students' AI literacy development, subject norms, anxiety, perceived usefulness of AI, AI for social good, attitude and confidence in using AI, and behavioral intention. These questions allowed teachers to investigate students' noncognitive perceptions toward AI literacy education. Sakulkueakulsuk et al. (2018) used surveys to evaluate students' accuracy rate of machine learning models to categorize the quality of mangoes throughout various

Table 7.4 Assessment constructs and tools to evaluate Students' AI Learning

Research methods	Constructs and tools (Ng et al., 2021b)	Some examples	Sample studies
Quantitative (14)	Use knowledge tests to assess students' AI cognitive gain and abilities	"What is the importance of similarity when clustering a dataset?"	Wan et al. (2020)
	Use perceived questionnaire to assess the noncognitive aspects, including perceived ability, confidence in using AI, intelligence, truthfulness, perceived understanding, subjective norms, AI anxiety, perceived usefulness of AI, AI for social good, attitude toward using AI, confidence in learning AI, learning behavioral intention, AI optimism, relevance, AI awareness, career adaptability skills	"The content of this AI class is relevant to my interests."	Chai et al. (2020), Chiu et al. (2021)
		"In this AI class, I prefer the materials that really challenge me so that I can learn new things."	
Qualitative (27)	Use videos, documents, pictures, presentations, students' interactions with AI agents and projects to examine students' AI cognitive and noncognitive abilities	"From students feedback, students reported that they were excited and happy to try an activity they've never tried before in a classroom and most had an underlying sense of sportsmanship to prove each other's views right/wrong"	Gunasilan (2021), Lee et al. (2021), Druga (2019)

stages, as well as other aspects such as futuristic thinking, engagement, interactivity, and interdisciplinary thinking.

Qualitative Methods To investigate students' satisfaction, motivations, and cognition levels, qualitative data was obtained through capturing students' work, field notes, project presentations, and interviews. Lee et al. (2021), for example, presented students' daily reflections and interviews about their workshop experiences in order to demonstrate their excitement while working on this activity. Students were also able to internalize their learning experience through interviews and relate to the ethical implications of technology design (e.g., How accurate is your model? What is the possibility for bias?), the challenges of learning AI, and their future job prospects (e.g., What will your future career be?). Sintov et al. (2016) designed a role-playing board game as a final project to reinforce students' decision-making.

Druga (2019) used field observations to record students' interactions with AI agents and a three-attribute AI perception questionnaire to assess how 102 children (7–12 years old) interacted with and perceived their AI agents in their lessons. These three attributes measure whether the agents are smarter, more trustworthy, and understand them (e.g., "What do you think of Google Voice, an AI-enabled agent?").

The most fun features, according to the children, were playing beatbox and music, taking pictures, and playing games. Gunasilan (2021) collected feedback after debate activities to reflect and refine the instruction design in terms of competitiveness, enjoyment, teamwork, self-reflection, and peer assessment in an evaluation session.

7.3 Conclusions

AI has grown popular and widely used across industries as a result of the fourth industrial revolution, owing to increased data volumes, advanced algorithms, and improvements in computing power and storage (Reed & Dongarra, 2015). Countries have begun to design and implement AI curricula to help students develop technology skills that will help them in their future studies and careers.

AI literacy is necessary to update the twenty-first century digital literacy skill sets for citizens and students so that they could be more competent and ready for their living, studies, and career in today's AI-driven world. After several years of implementation, AI curricula have been implemented to enable students to use AI knowledge and related technologies to facilitate their learning and build creations. This is the first review that summarizes the existing evidence of AI literacy education in secondary school settings in terms of research backgrounds, methodological approaches, pedagogical strategies used in the AI courses, learning tools that are used in the AI courses, learning content, assessment methods, and learning outcomes. We noticed that our findings were consistent with recent reviews (e.g., Ng et al., 2021a, b; Marques et al., 2020) that we could adapt the Bloom's taxonomy to understand the cognition gains of AI knowledge, concepts, and skills, as well as the TPACK model to understand the instructional design of selecting appropriate technologies/tools, pedagogies, and learning contents to teach students AI. Furthermore, in the twenty-first century competencies that bring up with digital citizens in today's global community, we identified important competences such as the 4Cs (communication, collaboration, critical thinking, and creativity). Students need to be able to communicate and create their thoughts, ideas, and solutions in order to solve future challenges and boost their competitiveness, in addition to knowing AI concepts and using AI applications ethically. This review contributes to providing a summary of the up-to-date literature to inform researchers, policymakers, and educators about how to effectively develop students' AI literacy at the pre-tertiary level.

Several limitations were noted, first, because the majority of the publications (21) were conference papers and half of the articles (15) used qualitative research methodologies. It was acknowledged that AI literacy is still an emerging issue and the majority of study was exploratory in nature. We foresee that future research design will shift to be more empirical and use rigorous research methods (e.g., quasi-experiment, design-based research) using interventions and control groups. A more comprehensive data analysis (e.g., t-test, ANOVA, factor analysis, regression, structural equation modeling) should be used. Second, there are few questionnaires available to evaluate secondary students' AI literacy, and none of them have been validated. Future study should focus on developing AI literacy measures, such as surveys and questionnaires, and assessing the scales' reliability and validity. Finally, establishing theoretical and pedagogical frameworks to assist policymakers, educators, and instructional designers with age-appropriate pedagogies, learning artifacts, and assessment methods must be prioritized in order to advance this research field.

References

Chai, C. S., Lin, P. Y., Jong, M. S. Y., Dai, Y., Chiu, T. K., & Huang, B. (2020, August). Factors influencing students; behavioral intention to continue artificial intelligence learning. In *2020 International Symposium on Educational Technology (ISET)* (pp. 147–150). IEEE.

Chai, C. S., Lin, P. Y., Jong, M. S. Y., Dai, Y., Chiu, T. K., & Qin, J. (2021). Perceptions of and behavioral intentions towards learning artificial intelligence in primary school students. *Educational Technology & Society, 24*(3), 89–101.

Chiu, T. K., Meng, H., Chai, C. S., King, I., Wong, S., & Yam, Y. (2021). Creation and evaluation of a pretertiary artificial intelligence (AI) curriculum. *IEEE Transactions on Education., 65*, 30–39.

Deng, W., Huang, X., Liu, Q., & Wang, Z. (2021, December). Curriculum design of artificial intelligence in middle school-taking posture recognition as an example. In *2021 Tenth International Conference of Educational Innovation Through Technology (EITT)* (pp. 310–315). IEEE.

Druga, S., Vu, S. T., Likhith, E., & Qiu, T. (2019). Inclusive AI literacy for kids around the world. In *Proceedings of FabLearn 2019* (pp. 104–111).

Estevez, J., Garate, G., & Graña, M. (2019). Gentle introduction to artificial intelligence for high-school students using scratch. *IEEE Access, 7*, 179027–179036.

Fernández-Martínez, C., Hernán-Losada, I., & Fernández, A. (2021). Early introduction of AI in Spanish middle schools. A motivational study. *KI-Künstliche Intelligenz, 35*(2), 163–170.

Gao, J., & Wang, L. (2019, August). Reverse thinking teaching discussion in high school information technology under new curriculum standards. In *2019 14th International Conference on Computer Science & Education (ICCSE)* (pp. 222–226). IEEE.

Glaser, B. G. (1965). The constant comparative method of qualitative analysis. *Social Problems, 12*(4), 436–445.

Gong, X., Wu, Y., Ye, Z., & Liu, X. (2018, June). Artificial intelligence course design: iSTREAM-based visual cognitive smart vehicles. In *2018 IEEE Intelligent Vehicles Symposium (IV)* (pp. 1731–1735). IEEE.

Gunasilan, U. (2021). Debate as a learning activity for teaching programming: A case in the subject of machine learning. *Higher Education, Skills and Work-based Learning, 12*, 705–718.

Kahn, K. M., Megasari, R., Piantari, E., & Junaeti, E. (2018). *AI programming by children using snap! Block programming in a developing country.* Retrieved from https://ecraft2learn. github.io/ai/publications/EC-TEL_2018_source-files_48%20kk%20edits%20changes%20 accepted.pdf

Kaspersen, M. H., Bilstrup, K. E. K., Van Mechelen, M., Hjorth, A., Bouvin, N. O., & Petersen, M. G. (2021, June). VotestratesML: A high school learning tool for exploring machine learning and its societal implications. In *FabLearn Europe/MakeEd 2021-An international conference on computing, design and making in education* (pp. 1–10).

Lee, I., Ali, S., Zhang, H., DiPaola, D., & Breazeal, C. (2021). Developing middle school students' AI literacy. In *Proceedings of the 52nd ACM technical symposium on computer science education* (pp. 191–197).

Marques, L. S., Gresse von Wangenheim, C., & Hauck, J. C. (2020). Teaching machine learning in school: A systematic mapping of the state of the art. *Informatics in Education, 19*(2), 283–321.

Morris, T. H. (2020). Experiential learning–a systematic review and revision of Kolb's model. *Interactive Learning Environments, 28*(8), 1064–1077.

Ng, D. T. K., & Chu, S. K. W. (2021). Motivating students to learn AI through social networking sites: A case study in Hong Kong. *Online Learning, 25*(1), 195–208.

Ng, D. T. K., Leung, J. K. L., Chu, K. W. S., & Qiao, M. S. (2021a). AI literacy: Definition, teaching, evaluation and ethical issues. *Proceedings of the Association for Information Science and Technology, 58*(1), 504–509.

Ng, D. T. K., Leung, J. K. L., Chu, S. K. W., & Qiao, M. S. (2021b). Conceptualizing AI literacy: An exploratory review. *Computers and Education: Artificial Intelligence, 2*, 100041.

Norouzi, N., Chaturvedi, S., & Rutledge, M. (2020, April). Lessons learned from teaching machine learning and natural language processing to high school students. In *Proceedings of the AAAI conference on artificial intelligence* (vol. 34, no. 09, pp. 13397–13403).

Reed, D. A., & Dongarra, J. (2015). Exascale computing and big data. *Communications of the ACM, 58*(7), 56–68.

Reyes, A. A., Elkin, C., Niyaz, Q., Yang, X., Paheding, S., & Devabhaktuni, V. K. (2020, August). A Preliminary work on visualization-based education tool for high school machine learning education. In *2020 IEEE Integrated STEM Education Conference (ISEC)* (pp. 1–5). IEEE.

Rodríguez-García, J. D., Moreno-León, J., Román-González, M., & Robles, G. (2020, October). Introducing artificial intelligence fundamentals with LearningML: artificial intelligence made easy. In *Eighth international conference on technological ecosystems for enhancing multiculturality* (pp. 18–20).

Sabuncuoglu, A. (2020). Designing one year curriculum to teach artificial intelligence for middle school. In *Proceedings of the 2020 ACM conference on innovation and technology in computer science education* (pp. 96–102).

Sakulkueakulsuk, B., Witoon, S., Ngarmkajornwiwat, P., Pataranutaporn, P., Surareungchai, W., Pataranutaporn, P., & Subsoontorn, P. (2018, December). Kids making AI: Integrating machine learning, gamification, and social context in STEM education. In *2018 IEEE international conference on Teaching, Assessment, and Learning for Engineering (TALE)* (pp. 1005–1010). IEEE.

Sanusi, I. T., Oyelere, S. S., Agbo, F. J., & Suhonen, J. (2021, October). Survey of resources for introducing machine learning in K-12 context. In *2021 IEEE Frontiers in Education Conference (FIE)* (pp. 1–9). IEEE.

Sintov, N., Kar, D., Nguyen, T., Fang, F., Hoffman, K., Lyet, A., & Tambe, M. (2016, March). From the lab to the classroom and beyond: extending a game-based research platform for teaching AI to diverse audiences. In *Proceedings of the AAAI Conference on Artificial Intelligence* (Vol. 30, No. 1).

Tamborg, A. L., Elicer, R., & Spikol, D. (2022). Programming and computational thinking in mathematics education. *KI-Künstliche Intelligenz*, 1–9.

Touretzky, D., Gardner-McCune, C., Martin, F., & Seehorn, D. (2019, July). Envisioning AI for K-12: What should every child know about AI? In *Proceedings of the AAAI conference on artificial intelligence* (vol. 33, no. 01, pp. 9795–9799).

UNESCO. (2022). *K-12 AI curricula: A mapping of government-endorsed AI curricula.* Retrieved from https://unesdoc.unesco.org/ark:/48223/pf0000380602

Vachovsky, M. E., Wu, G., Chaturapruek, S., Russakovsky, O., Sommer, R., & Fei-Fei, L. (2016, February). Toward more gender diversity in CS through an artificial intelligence summer program for high school girls. In *Proceedings of the 47th ACM technical symposium on computing science education* (pp. 303–308).

Wan, X., Zhou, X., Ye, Z., Mortensen, C. K., & Bai, Z. (2020, June). SmileyCluster: Supporting accessible machine learning in K-12 scientific discovery. In *Proceedings of the interaction design and children conference* (pp. 23–35).

Zhang, J., & Du, H. (2008, December). The PBL's application research on prolog language's instruction. In *2008 international workshop on education technology and training & 2008 international workshop on geoscience and remote sensing* (vol. 1, pp. 112–114). IEEE.

Zimmermann-Niefield, A., Turner, M., Murphy, B., Kane, S. K., & Shapiro, R. B. (2019, June). Youth learning machine learning through building models of athletic moves. In *Proceedings of the 18th ACM international conference on interaction design and children* (pp. 121–132).

Chapter 8
AI Literacy Education for Nonengineering Undergraduates

AI literacy is in high demand across industries. Thus, being literate in or learning AI should no longer be viewed as a specialized field under engineering but an ability that penetrates all disciplines (Johri, 2020). An analogy to extend this argument is by viewing traditional literacy. We would expect not only linguistics students to be competent in literacy, which is the proficiency to read and write, but also an appropriate level of literacy across any majors. Similarly, students at all levels and disciplines should develop AI literacy to stay competent in today's world.

In previous chapters, reviews had presented the educational levels across several years as a single unit (i.e., kindergarten, primary school, and secondary school). However, when it comes to postsecondary level, this unification becomes inapplicable. Students acquire knowledge and develop competencies toward their profession. The curricula focus on specialized subject domains instead of foundational and whole-person development as in K–12. Though one may argue about the shift in the twenty-first century educational paradigm where higher education is being remodeled to a more dynamic and interdisciplinary state, one of the core objectives of universities remains to be helping students progress into employment, which primarily is still driven by their major studies. And hence, it is more logical to continue the review of AI literacy education in postsecondary level by differentiating the students' major of study.

But where should we draw the line? What we would like to investigate is whether, and to what extent, there is an emergence of AI literacy education even though the majors "traditionally" do not involve AI. One possibility is to separate AI majors from all other programs. However, the coverage of AI literacy may spread beyond AI-specific courses. For example, a command in programming contributes to partial steps to understand, apply, and create AI, but the introduction to programming, for instance, is also a typical subject for computer science or even engineering students. We also found examples where universities have proposed to make AI education mandatory regardless of the students' discipline (de Freitas & Weingart, 2021). Therefore, there is no definite line to draw in this respect. As this chapter will

D. T. K. Ng et al., *AI Literacy in K-16 Classrooms*,
https://doi.org/10.1007/978-3-031-18880-0_8

explain, a general term, nonengineering undergraduates (NEU in short) is used. The review uses various approaches in an attempt to capture more evidence on how educators design learning experiences for NEUs to develop AI literacy.

Many universities are not new to offering programs on AI, but most of them are exclusive for computer science (CS) majors, CS-related engineering students or offered to postgraduates (Mishra & Siy, 2020). The literature signifies the trends and importance of AI education at all levels, while the AI curriculum development for NEUs is under-explored. This chapter aims to shed light on the instructional design, pedagogies, learning artifacts, and the topic areas on AI literacy mentioned in discussion papers and empirical studies related to NEUs. Most research on this similar topic focuses on K–12, and thus a research gap lies in the current state for NEUs. This study also represents an extension to Ng et al.' (2021) work on AI literacy at different education levels. In their study, only four articles were identified in the category of higher education. This study aims to broaden the search by including more databases and to be more specific to literature that focuses on NEUs. This study aims to answer the following questions:

RQ1: What pedagogies have been used in teaching AI to NEUs?
RQ2: What aspects of AI literacy have NEUs developed?
RQ3: What learning artifacts have been used in teaching AI to NEUs?

8.1 Methodology

8.1.1 Data Collection

Both electronic databases search and snowball sampling were undertaken in search for publications within our scope. For database search, relevant peer-reviewed articles and conference papers were identified from five world's trusted databases, namely, Web of Science, Scopus, ERICs, ProQuest, and IEEE. The selected databases ensure the inclusion of evidence-based quality research (Mongeon & Paul-Hus, 2016). There were two sets of search phrases. The first set included "AI" OR "artificial intelligence" OR "artificial intelligence literacy" OR "deep learning" OR "machine learning" OR "neural network*" OR "intelligent agent"; the other set included "non-computer science majors" OR "nonmajors" OR "nonengineering." Matched results in either the title, abstract, or keywords were downloaded. As of 16 April 2022, 507 records were identified. After the process of initial screening (462), removing duplicate studies and those unable to access full text (18), and excluding studies that were not targeted to NEUs or not related to AI education (15), 12 articles were included for detailed review.

For snowball sampling, it is a non-probability sampling technique that uses the initial set of samples to introduce, refer, and generate further samples (Parker et al., 2019). Based on the references from the included articles, eight more articles were included by chain referencing. As a result, 20 articles were reviewed. The search protocol is summarized using the PRISMA diagram presented in Fig. 8.1.

RQ2 concerns a mapping of what and how AI was taught as described in the articles into aspects of AI literacy. As illustrated in the UNESCO report, AI literacy comprises both data literacy and algorithm literacy, and it serves as an orientation of "knowledge, understanding, skills, and value of AI" (UNESCO, 2022, p. 11). Three main categories of AI curriculum content were proposed which were further divided into nine topic areas. We adopted the AI curriculum areas suggested in the UNESCO report and developed a coding system according to the topic areas as illustrated in Table 8.1.

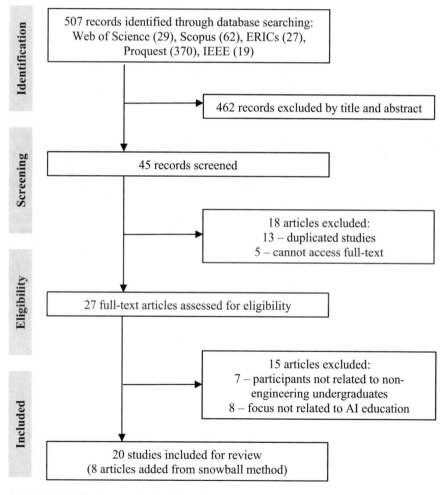

Fig. 8.1 PRISMA diagram of included articles

Table 8.1 Coding system of AI literacy topic area

Category	Topic area	Code
AI foundations	Algorithms and programming	A1
	Data literacy	A2
	Contextual problem-solving	A3
Ethics and social impact	The ethics of AI	B1
	The social or societal implications of AI	B2
	Applications of AI to domains other than ICT	B3
Understanding, using, and developing AI	Understanding and using AI techniques	C1
	Understanding and using AI technologies	C2
	Developing AI technologies	C3

Adapted from UNESCO (2021)

8.1.2   Data Analysis

We conducted document analysis to review and evaluate its content systematically (Bowen, 2009). The procedure in this study involved an iterative process of (1) identifying relevant program information, (2) categorizing and coding the content, (3) interpreting the patterns of program description, and (4) sorting into themes. To ensure coding reliability, six articles were randomly picked, blind-coded, and analyzed by two researchers. Agreements were reached for any discrepancies in the understanding of the coding systems before moving forward to thorough analysis.

Table 8.2 shows the characteristics of the reviewed articles by their published year, country, type of article, and research methods. As mentioned above, there is an increasing attention to AI education in recent years, and the growing number of publications since 2016 is in line with this notion. Moreover, the jump is even more notable in the year 2021. This is a positive indication that more scholars are putting effort in discussing AI for nonengineering majors. For the origins of the publication, the majority of the articles published were from the United States. In terms of research methods, there is an even spread of qualitative (5), quantitative (6), and mixed-method (2) papers. Conceptual papers (6) refer to articles that the scholars tend to share their insights toward the area and their experiences and good practices in their teaching.

8.2   Results and Discussion

RQ1: What pedagogies were used in teaching AI to NEUs?

The pedagogies described in the reviewed articles are summarized in Table 8.3. Most studies used project-based or hands-on experiential learning in their courses to teach AI to NEUs. Most projects involved learning artifacts which aid problems or advancements of students' subject domain by introducing possibilities with AI. For

Table 8.2 Frequency (N, %) of the characteristics of the reviewed articles

Variables	Categories	N	Percent (%)
Year	<2010	3	15
	2016	2	10
	2017	2	10
	2018	1	5
	2019	3	15
	2020	1	5
	2021	6	30
	2022	2	10
Countries	Austria	1	5
	Canada	2	10
	China	2	10
	Hong Kong	1	5
	Portugal	1	5
	South Korea	2	10
	Taiwan	2	10
	United States	9	45
Types of articles	Journal articles	9	45
	Conference papers	11	55
Research methods	Qualitative	5	25
	Quantitative	6	30
	Mixed research	2	10
	Conceptual papers	6	30
	Not mentioned	1	5

example, Armstrong (2010) introduced two autonomous robots in his course. The instructors removed the robots' outer shells to let students explore the mechanical components and the controlling sensors. After students learned about the exteroceptive and proprioceptive sensors on both, they were tasked with programming tasks to learn about intelligent systems and related topics. A more recent study by Lin et al. (2021) introduced hands-on exercises to train an AI model that could identify directions and use the model to control a motor-controlled car.

A few studies used games and competitions to motivate students' interest to learn AI. For example, Rattadilok et al. (2018) developed an intervention named In-Class Gamified Machine Learning Environment (iGaME) based on a mobile game called Clash of Clans. Results showed that students engaging in games can enable key machine learning concepts. The gamified platform also made customized learning experiences possible. Another study which also combined gamification and competition-based learning is by de Freitas and Weingart (2021). NEUs in their course programmed a rocket landing simulator using Python. Students competed by applying genetic algorithms to train the rocket to land in the safest and most efficient manner. Their findings indicated that NEUs can understand AI concepts

Table 8.3 Descriptive information of the included studies

Author/ year	Article title	Type of study	Research design	Participant	Pedagogy	Learning artifacts	Key findings and notions	AI literacy
Armstrong (2010)	Robotics and intelligent systems for social and behavioral science undergraduates	Empirical	Not mentioned	Not mentioned	Experiential learning, project-based	Robotics, ActionScript, Python	Leveraging the appeal of robotics and artificial intelligence to improve recruitment to the major and to expose students in other disciplines to computational thinking	A1, A3, C2
Au-Yong-Oliveira et al. (2020)	What can we expect from the future? The impact of artificial intelligence on society	Discussion	Questionnaire and interviews	110 mixed engineering and nonengineering students	N/A	N/A	AI may lead to negative impact on work and loss of control. Humans will be ahead of AI. Engineering students are more afraid of AI than nonengineering students	B1, B2, B3

Danyluk (2004)	Using robotics to motivate learning in an AI course for non-majors	Discussion	N/A	N/A	Experiential learning, project-based	Robotics, LEGO, Handyboard, C, light sensors	The lab provides a setting in which students can build confidence; the fun of working with robots motivates students to be more engaged in lecture; and students learn some fundamental programming concepts in addition to material about AI	A1, C2
de Freitas and Weingart (2021)	I'm Going to Learn What?!? Teaching Artificial Intelligence to Freshmen in an Introductory Computer Science Course	Empirical	Assignment performance and questionnaire	174 freshmen	Competition-based	Python, teachable machine	Non-computer scientists can comprehend AI/ML concepts without being overwhelmed by the subject material	A1, A3, B1, B2, C1, C2
Eaton et al. (2017)	Blue sky ideas in artificial intelligence education from the EAAI 2017 new and future AI educator program	Discussion	N/A	N/A	Peer learning	N/A	Using seminar-style approach or project-based approach to connect subject students with AI students	A3

(continued)

Table 8.3 (continued)

Author/year	Article title	Type of study	Research design	Participant	Pedagogy	Learning artifacts	Key findings and notions	AI literacy
Fox (2007)	Finding the "Right" Robot Competition: Targeting Non-Engineering Undergraduates	Empirical	Not mentioned	Four to six teams from three to four schools	Competition-based, gamified learning	LEGO, Handyboard	There are relatively fewer competitions suitable for NEUs to introduce them to AI or robotics techniques	A1, C2
Gil (2016)	Teaching Big Data Analytics Skills with Intelligent Workflow Systems	Discussion	N/A	N/A	Experiential learning	WINGS intelligent workflow system	Students will be able to get firsthand experiences with a breadth of big data topics, including multistep data analytic and statistical methods, software reuse and composition, parallel distributed programming, high-end computing	A1, A2, C2
Hu and Wang (2021)	Study on Teaching Reform of Artificial Intelligence Education in non-Computer Major	Discussion	N/A	N/A	N/A	N/A	AI experiences a low development process and fails to attract attention. The popularization of AI education in non-computer major involves the adjustment of the whole information general education system	A1, A2, C1

Kandlhofer et al. (2016)	Artificial intelligence and computer science in education: From kindergarten to university	Empirical	Observations and interviews	N/A	Constructionism, demonstrative hands-on activities	Golog, YAGI, Unity	All students successfully completed the course and gained deeper understanding of AI topics and a higher abstraction level	A3, C2
Kim and Shim (2022)	Development of an AR-Based AI Education App for Non-Majors	Empirical	Questionnaires	88 nonengineering undergraduates	AR-based AI education for visually hands-on experiences	Unity, AIEduAR, QR code	Based on TAM and IMMS results, students are highly likely to accept and learn AR technology in AI education	A1, A3, C1, C2
Kong et al. (2021)	Evaluation of an artificial intelligence literacy course for university students with diverse study backgrounds	Empirical	Questionnaire and interviews	120 mixed nonmajors	Flipped classroom	Not mentioned	Students without prior knowledge of programming could understand AI concepts of machine learning, supervised learning, regression, classification, unsupervised learning, and clustering	A1, A3, B1, B2, B3, C1

(continued)

Table 8.3 (continued)

Author/ year	Article title	Type of study	Research design	Participant	Pedagogy	Learning artifacts	Key findings and notions	AI literacy
Lee and Cho (2021)	Development of an Artificial Intelligence Education Model of Classification Techniques for Non-computer Majors	Empirical	Questionnaire and AI comprehension test	11 non-computer majors	Experiential learning	Python, teachable machine	Perception and understanding of AI were correlated with education satisfaction	A1, A2, B2, B3, C2
Li (2019)	Experience Report: Explorable Web Apps to Teach AI to NonMajors	Empirical	Qualitative student feedback	mixed of CS and nontechnical students (# not mentioned)	Explorable explanations, interactive illustrations, self-guided discoveries	Course Catalog Prerequisite Extraction, Pattern-Matching Chatbot, Bayesian Network Calculator	The presentation of CS content to non-CS students have benefited from use of interactive web apps that allow students to explore CS concepts without writing code	A1, C1, C2
Lin et al. (2021)	STEM-based Artificial Intelligence Learning in General Education for NonEngineering Undergraduate Students	Empirical	Questionnaires	328 nonengineering freshmen	Project-based	Custom Vision (deep learning), Raspberry Pi (robot car)	AI literacy is correlated to their awareness of AI ethical issues. STEM-based AI curriculum increased the awareness of AI ethical issues among low-AI-literate learners	B1, B2, C2

Rattadilok et al. (2018)	Teaching Students About Machine Learning Through a Gamified Approach	Empirical	Assignment performance	Not mentioned	Gamified learning, universal design for learning, personalized learning	iGaME	Students engaging in games can enable key machine learning concepts. Games can customize learning experiences	C1, C2
Shih et al. (2021)	Learning Ethics in AI—Teaching Non-Engineering Undergraduates through Situated Learning	Empirical	Questionnaires	328 nonengineering freshmen	Situated learning	Custom vision (deep learning), Raspberry Pi (robot car)	A strong link between AI understanding and attitudes and AI ethics	B1, B2, C2
Sulmont et al. (2019a)	What Is Hard About Teaching Machine Learning to Non-Majors? Insights from Classifying Instructors' Learning Goals	Empirical	Interview	10 instructors	N/A	Scikit-learn, Microsoft Azure Machine Learning	Learning goals, such as making design decisions and comparing/contrasting models, are difficult to teach. Learning goals are consistent with the levels of the Structure of Observed Learning Outcomes (SOLO) taxonomy	A1, A2, A3, C1

(continued)

Table 8.3 (continued)

Author/ year	Article title	Type of study	Research design	Participant	Pedagogy	Learning artifacts	Key findings and notions	AI literacy
Sulmont et al. (2019b)	Can You Teach Me To Machine Learn?	Empirical	Structured Interview	10 instructors	N/A	N/A	Student preconceptions include ideas that ML is important, but also not accessible. [...] it is possible to teach ML to those with little to no math/CS background. [...] students having difficulty appreciating the human decision-making aspects of ML, and overestimating the power of ML to solve real-world problems	A1, A2, A3, C1
Way et al. (2017)	Machine learning modules for all disciplines	Discussion	N/A	N/A	Problem-based	WEKA (Text Classification)	12 modules are designed for use in a variety of educational scenarios. Students experience solid learning that is retained and nontechnical students generally gain more than technical students	A1, A2, A3, C1

Yang et al. (2021)	Stakeholders' perspectives on the future of artificial intelligence in radiology: a scoping review	Review	Document analysis	62 publications	N/A	N/A	A significant impact on radiology but unlikely replacing radiologists. Non-computer scientists have limited AI knowledge. Collaboration between radiologists and AI specialists is needed	B1, B2, B3

without a strong background in computer science and that students acknowledged the importance and value of learning AI through their course.

Within the popular approach of using project-based learning to teach AI, we speculate a shift in the type of projects introduced in the courses. While the projects before 2010 tended to link AI with robots, recent studies tended to make use of practical applications in the specific disciplines. This phenomenon may be explained by what drove educators to teach AI to NEUs. In early to mid-2000s, there was a decline in enrollments in computer science departments, and hence the objective was only to use AI topics to attract students' interest (e.g., Danyluk, 2004; Fox, 2007). At present, applications of AI are penetrated in most disciplines, and therefore educators are embedding AI literacy into part of students' subject curriculum (e.g., Kim & Shim, 2022; Kong et al., 2021).

RQ2: What aspects of AI literacy had NEUs developed?

The mapping of AI topic areas is shown in the rightmost column of Table 8.3. Some articles (e.g., Au-Yong-Oliveira et al., 2020; Eaton et al., 2018) did not center discussions on the types of AI content but other issues such as instructional strategies and learners' perceptions. The following discussion is guided based on three categories: AI foundations, ethics and social impact, and understanding, using and developing AI (UNESCO, 2021).

For AI foundations, most articles (12) covered topics related to algorithms and programming (A1), which represent teaching of basic technical engagement with AI. However, only five articles discussed the instructions for data literacy (A2) and seven used project-based learning as their key pedagogy to solve problems in disciplinary-specific contexts (A3). Most studies (e.g., Kong et al., 2021) designed instructions such that prior knowledge of computer science or programming was not necessary. Hence, it is reasonable that instructors choose the minimal level of AI foundations needed for their students to experience AI.

For ethics and social impact, we see an interesting divide by the year of publication that is similar to our argument in RQ1. Most recently published articles (e.g., Au-Yong-Oliveira et al., 2020; Kong et al., 2021) would address the balance between the convenience that AI brings to our daily lives as well as the potential threats and ethical challenges if AI is not implemented properly. Studies earlier than 2010 hardly mentioned any concerns for ethical considerations. The attention to this aspect would only seem to increase in proportion to the rapid development of AI applications across industries and in our daily lives.

For understanding, using, and developing AI, most studies (12) used AI technologies (C2) as a service to address the needs in the field of NEUs. As students experienced these technologies, some instructors would explain the AI techniques (C1) behind such that students could try to practice applying the service or replicating the results on their own. Finally, none of the studies reported to teach their students to develop AI technologies (C3). This is not surprising as the target audience is NEUs and the learning objectives were to understand basic concepts or to apply AI in their disciplines, rather than reaching a higher level of mastery.

RQ3: What learning artifacts were used in teaching AI to NEUs?

In order to teach AI to those with little background knowledge in mathematics and programming, using tools to visualize what AI or ML can do is a popular and practical tactic (Sulmont et al., 2019b). Similar to previous chapters, instructors choose the types of learning artifacts which match students' learning goals and available resources. These artifacts can be categorized into hardware-focused, software-focused, and intelligent agents. The definitions and the categorization of these learning artifacts are shown in Table 8.4.

For hardware-focused artifacts, using robotics is a straightforward representation of what AI can achieve. Students can build robots to achieve certain mechanical tasks such as pathfinding by sensors or performing object sorting by image recognition. For example, Fox (2007) used LEGO-based robots as the tool to attract NEUs to participate in an AI-related competition. A couple of limitations were mentioned as NEUs do not have the necessary knowhow to understand and build such sophisticated machines. So, there was a continuous struggle between not setting expectations too high and providing sufficient autonomy for students to explore the possibilities. One observation from this review is that few recent articles mentioned using hardware-focused artifacts as their teaching tool. A possible explanation is because the focus of AI has shifted from highly associated with humanoid robots in the early 2000s to the wide range of app-based applications.

For software-focused artifacts, some articles reported using Python as the AI programming platform. de Freitas and Weingart (2021) taught students to use Python to write a program for a rocket landing simulator. In the assignment, students needed to use AI to generate random locations for the rocket, to track performance indicators such as fuel consumption and velocity of the rocket, and to design controls for the rocket's thrusters for successful landing. In another example, Way et al. (2017) proposed several teaching ideas using WEKA Text Classification for NEUs: art majors were engaged in a classification and clustering module; French

Table 8.4 Learning artifacts mentioned in the reviewed articles

	Definition	Learning artifacts examples	Sample studies
Hardware-focused artifacts	Use physical artifacts to learn AI such as robotics, sensors and Arduino devices	Robotics, LEGO, Handyboard, light sensors, Raspberry Pi	Armstrong (2010), Danyluk (2004), Fox (2007)
Software-focused artifacts	Use digital artifacts to learn AI such as block/syntax-based programming and simulation	Python, ActionScript, C, Custom Vision (deep learning), WEKA (Text Classification), C++	de Freitas and Weingart (2021), Lee and Cho (2021), Lin et al. (2021)
Intelligent agents	Use intelligent agents such as expert systems, machine learning trainers, chatbots to build their custom machine learning models without coding	Teachable Machine, Golog, YAGI, Unity, AIEduAR, Course Catalog Prerequisite Extraction, Pattern-Matching Chatbot, Bayesian Network Calculator, iGaME, Scikit-learn, Microsoft Azure Machine Learning	Rattadilok et al. (2018), Sulmont et al. (2019a), Kandlhofer et al. (2016)

literature students could learn about AI Machine Translation embedded in their writing and stylistics course.

The key difference between software-focused artifacts and intelligent agents is that the former involves learners in the analytical, mathematical, or algorithmic processes of AI. Leaners can use the software artifacts to understand, apply, or create the "thinking" processes of AI, whereas the latter focuses only on using a packaged platform or technology for applications without coding. Rattadilok et al. (2018) had successfully engaged students in a gamified AI learning experience which enhanced students' machine learning concepts. They developed an intelligent agent named iGaME (In-Class Gamified Machine learning Environment) for teaching machine learning algorithms with the adaptation of an online strategy mobile game called Clash of Clans. They compared teaching with iGaME to traditional machine learning teaching and suggested the use of intelligent agents could motivate nontechnical students to study difficult technologically driven topics such as machine learning and AI.

8.3 Conclusion

Artificial intelligence (AI) is widely applied in almost any industry, such as manufacturing, economy, communications, transportation, information, finance, education, medical care, etc. (Pan, 2018; Sestino & De Mauro, 2022). Researchers and educators are in search of ways to define and upskill students' AI literacy. However, few studies have visited how NEUs can be introduced to and be literate in AI. In the form of a review, this chapter consolidated the available publications that address this gap.

The review used database search and snowball sampling and resulted in 20 articles that targeted their discussions on AI for NEUs. Project-based learning and hands-on experiences were found to be the most commonly adopted approaches by instructors. The content described in the articles was mapped into nine topic areas adapted from the UNESCO report (UNESCO, 2021). The learning artifacts that aided the teaching of AI were categorized into hardware, software, and intelligent agents focused.

Notwithstanding, there are a few limitations of this study that should be noted. First, it was difficult to capture all studies on non-computer majors as there was not a unified terminology for this group of students. Some studies did not include any term such as non-computer scientists or nontechnical students in their studies. For example, Yang et al. (2021) elicited perspectives from radiology students which were also included in this review. Second, there are a noticeably increasing number of online, self-paced AI programs offered by universities for diverse audiences. It is highly possible that these programs will gain popularity among NEUs. Future study is needed to elicit the impact of these programs on learners' AI literacy. The study benefits future educators who intend to design AI learning programs that target NEUs. This review also contributes to the broader scope of AI literacy development of students at all educational levels.

References

Armstrong, T. (2010, June). Robotics and intelligent systems for social and behavioral science undergraduates. In *Proceedings of the fifteenth annual conference on Innovation and technology in computer science education* (pp. 194–198).

Au-Yong-Oliveira, M., Lopes, C., Soares, F., Pinheiro, G., & Guimarães, P. (2020, June). What can we expect from the future? The impact of artificial intelligence on society. In *2020 15th Iberian Conference on Information Systems and Technologies (CISTI)* (pp. 1–6). IEEE.

Bowen, G. A. (2009). Document analysis as a qualitative research method. *Qualitative Research Journal, 9*, 27.

Danyluk, A. (2004, March). Using robotics to motivate learning in an AI course for non-majors. In *AAAI spring symposium* (pp. 22–24).

de Freitas, A. A., & Weingart, T. B. (2021, March). I'm going to learn what? Teaching artificial intelligence to freshmen in an introductory computer science course. In *Proceedings of the 52nd ACM technical symposium on computer science education* (pp. 198–204).

Eaton, E., Koenig, S., Schulz, C., Maurelli, F., Lee, J., Eckroth, J., et al. (2018). Blue sky ideas in artificial intelligence education from the EAAI 2017 new and future AI educator program. *AI Matters, 3*(4), 23–31.

Fox, S. E. (2007). Finding the "Right" Robot competition: Targeting non-engineering undergraduates. In *AAAI spring symposium: Semantic scientific knowledge integration* (pp. 49–52).

Gil, Y. (2016, March). Teaching big data analytics skills with intelligent workflow systems. In *Proceedings of the AAAI conference on artificial intelligence* (vol. 30, no. 1).

Hu, Q., & Wang, K. (2021, August). Study on teaching reform of artificial intelligence education in non-computer major. In *The Sixth international conference on information management and technology* (pp. 1–4).

Johri, A. (2020). Artificial intelligence and engineering education. *Journal of Engineering Education, 3*, 358–361.

Kandlhofer, M., Steinbauer, G., Hirschmugl-Gaisch, S., & Huber, P. (2016, October). Artificial intelligence and computer science in education: From kindergarten to university. In *2016 IEEE Frontiers in Education Conference (FIE)* (pp. 1–9). IEEE.

Kim, J., & Shim, J. (2022). Development of an AR-based AI education app for non-majors. *IEEE Access, 10*, 14149–14156.

Kong, S. C., Cheung, W. M. Y., & Zhang, G. (2021). Evaluation of an artificial intelligence literacy course for university students with diverse study backgrounds. *Computers and Education: Artificial Intelligence, 2*, 100026.

Lee, Y., & Cho, J. (2021). Development of an artificial intelligence education model of classification techniques for non-computer majors. *JOIV: International Journal on Informatics Visualization, 5*(2), 113–119.

Li, J. (2019). Experience report: Explorable web apps to teach AI to non-majors. *Journal of Computing Sciences in Colleges, 34*(4), 128–133.

Lin, C. H., Yu, C. C., Shih, P. K., & Wu, L. Y. (2021). STEM based Artificial Intelligence Learning in General Education for Non-Engineering Undergraduate Students. *Educational Technology & Society, 24*(3), 224–237.

Mishra, A., & Siy, H. (2020, October). An interdisciplinary approach for teaching artificial intelligence to computer science students. In *Proceedings of the 21st annual conference on information technology education* (pp. 344–344).

Mongeon, P., & Paul-Hus, A. (2016). The journal coverage of Web of Science and Scopus: a comparative analysis. *Scientometrics, 106*(1), 213–228.

Ng, D. T. K., Leung, J. K. L., Chu, S. K. W., & Qiao, M. S. (2021). Conceptualizing AI literacy: An exploratory review. *Computers and Education: Artificial Intelligence, 2*, 100041.

Pan, Y. H. (2018). 2018 special issue on artificial intelligence 2.0: Theories and applications. *Frontiers of Information Technology & Electronic Engineering, 19*(1), 1–2.

Parker, C., Scott, S., & Geddes, A. (2019). Snowball sampling. In *SAGE research methods foundations*.

Rattadilok, P., Roadknight, C., & Li, L. (2018, December). Teaching students about machine learning through a gamified approach. In *2018 IEEE international conference on Teaching, Assessment, and Learning for Engineering (TALE)* (pp. 1011–1015). IEEE.

Sestino, A., & De Mauro, A. (2022). Leveraging artificial intelligence in business: Implications, applications and methods. *Technology Analysis & Strategic Management, 34*(1), 16–29.

Shih, P. K., Lin, C. H., Wu, L. Y. Y., & Yu, C. C. (2021). Learning ethics in AI – Teaching nonengineering undergraduates through situated learning. *Sustainability, 13*(7), 3718.

Sulmont, E., Patitsas, E., & Cooperstock, J. R. (2019a). What is hard about teaching machine learning to non-majors? Insights from classifying instructors' learning goals. *ACM Transactions on Computing Education (TOCE), 19*(4), 1–16.

Sulmont, E., Patitsas, E., & Cooperstock, J. R. (2019b). Can you teach me to machine learn? In *Proceedings of the 50th ACM technical symposium on computer science education* (pp. 948–954).

UNESCO. (2021). *Survey for mapping of AI curricula*. Unpublished (Submitted to UNESCO).

UNESCO. (2022). *K-12 AI curricula: A mapping of government-endorsed AI curricula*. Retrieved May 4, 2022, from https://www.unesco.org/en/articles/unesco-releases-report-mapping-k-12-artificial-intelligence-curricula

Way, T., Papalaskari, M. A., Cassel, L., Matuszek, P., Weiss, C., & Tella, Y. P. (2017, June). Machine learning modules for all disciplines. In *Proceedings of the 2017 ACM conference on innovation and technology in computer science education* (pp. 84–85).

Yang, L., Ene, I. C., Arabi Belaghi, R., Koff, D., Stein, N., & Santaguida, P. L. (2021). Stakeholders' perspectives on the future of artificial intelligence in radiology: A scoping review. *European Radiology*, 1–19.

Part III
AI Literacy for Instructional Designers

Chapter 9
AI Literacy on Human-Centered Considerations

Part II of this book gave us an overview of AI literacy across educational levels. Several models of AI literacy education, in particular Bloom's taxonomy, TPACK model, as well as the P21's Framework for the 21st Century Learning (2009) that comprises key digital competencies that inform instructional designers what knowledge, skills, and attitudes students should equip with.

Although these frames suggest useful instructional resources on a research level, there is a lack of discussion to inform developers within the industry and teachers at large about what particular digital competencies they need to facilitate their product or service development and teaching in classrooms, respectively. Artificial intelligence offers unprecedented opportunities for EdTech companies to develop AI-based products for K–12 and higher education institutions. However, EdTech startups and companies may have a broad sense of what the market desires yet not fully aware of teachers' and students' holistic needs when learning AI. As a result, many EdTech on AI education arises, but few can sustain and oftentimes only become a gimmick. On the other hand, educational institutions have started to design professional training programs for the teacher workforce to integrate AI applications throughout the student life cycle. For example, the MIT Schwarzman College of Computing considered humanistic perspectives as the keys for understanding the implications of computation for knowledge and representation, and connected AI to the critical process of how knowledge works in culture (MIT, 2019).

Part III (Chaps. 9 and 10) aims to explore how instructional designers (i.e., AI developers and teachers) prepare themselves to become ready to design developmentally appropriate tools, platforms, services, and curricula to empower students with AI literacy skills.

9.1   Overview

The first half of this part, Chap. 9, focuses more on the human-centered design and product developmental aspects of AI literacy education. Of which much of the emphasis is placed on the learning of human-centeredness of AI, i.e., human-centered AI (HCAI). To achieve this goal, both "what" content should be covered and "how" it should be taught are equally important. By foregrounding human-centeredness in AI, i.e., Sections 9.2 and 9.3, the content created with this basis can establish a future-proof foundation for students to appropriately embrace the impacts of AI. Then in Sect. 9.4, we focus on the pedagogical approach in order to scaffold students' literacies. AI, which was once an abstract, highly skilled subject, is now brought down to K–16 education. Careful implementation of instructional design is necessary for such learning experiences to be effective.

Based on the notions of HCAI, some design principles that place users and learners at the center are proposed to aid researchers and developers when designing such learning tools. Furthermore, the calls for HCAI that meet students' cognitive and social needs and the educational kits with considerations of ethical concerns behind have been rapidly emerging. The chapter will provide insights on the key issues to be taken into account when designing learning artifacts to help reinforce students' acquisition of AI literacy skills and facilitate their learning.

9.2   Needs of HCAI in Educational Fields

Nowadays, service and product providers have entered the educational sector to offer intelligent learning solutions for educators and students. Although these EdTech applications are innovation rich for the business models of providers and users, few attention has been paid to the role of human values in developing AI technology. Some scholars proposed the need to establish models and guidelines to place human values at the center of AI design and development (Dignum, 2019). The idea of human-centered design was first suggested to remind developers to put humans at the center of AI development, rather than considering AI as a replacement for human agency (Renz & Vladova, 2021; Xu, 2019). In the educational sector, some scholars started to propose the idea of HCAI to enhance teaching/learning experience. For example, Yang (2021) pointed out that learning technology must be human-centered because it involves teaching and interacting with people. Rather than focusing on students' performance, human feelings and outcomes should be a major concern in designing smart learning environments. Several key elements of human-centered considerations were identified in educational fields when developing appropriate tools and systems for students: human factors designs and values, human intelligence, ethical and responsible design, as well as AI under human control and under human conditions.

9.3   Key Elements of Human-Centered Considerations

9.3.1   Human Factor Designs and Values

The first framework of HCAI in educational fields is proposed by Xu (2019) who suggested three ideas regarding how human factor designs and human values are considered when designing and implementing AI learning technologies. First, these learning technologies need to be ethically designed that developers should avoid discrimination and ensure justice and fairness in their AI solutions (Xu, 2019). One possibility to achieve this is by adopting a design thinking approach during the development of AI applications and systems. Design thinking is an iterative process that developers need to empathize with users (e.g., teachers, students), define problems from users' perspectives, and create solutions by prototyping and testing (Dam & Siang, 2018). This is consistent with the notion for learner-centered design that is guided by a constructivist theory and advancements in computer-assisted technology. Learner-centered design focuses on the quality of student learning to enhance students' needs, interests, and goals (Webber, 2012). This led to student-centered learning that requires students to set their own learning goals and determine appropriate resources and activities that will facilitate them to meet those targets (Jonassen, 2000; Hannafin & Land, 2000). When learners pursue their own goals or enjoy their learning, their learning activities would become meaningful to them. For example, Dhungel et al. (2021) applied a human-centered approach to develop a MOOC about AI for civil servants. To understand whether this course is suitable for the target audiences, a learning analysis was conducted to examine their mindsets, knowledge gained, and attitudes to develop a set of learning units that ground the abstract AI topics in concrete case scenarios taken from the public sector. Civil servants need to have a practical understanding of AI including knowing the potentials, challenges, and limitations of AI, as well as when and how to use it ethically. Yang et al. (2021) proposed the idea of "precision education" that educators need to adapt to changes due to learning diversity in four steps: diagnosis, prediction, treatment, and prevention. Most tools and platforms have the problems with a one-size-fits-all approach because learners have different educational backgrounds. Educators should change their pedagogical approaches and apply teaching strategies and methods wisely to enhance students' learning outcomes.

9.3.2   Reflect Human Intelligence

Learning technologies should reflect human intelligence and consider human characteristics and needs in the algorithm and system design (Xu, 2019). For example, Pérez-Ortiz et al. (2021) applied a personalized learning companion using AI algorithms and software tools with the goal of making it intuitive and user-friendly, as well as making the AI transparent and explainable to the teachers and students. The tools combine AI and HCI to create an integrated suite of tools for teachers and learners to cognitively support them to work with the AI agents. In this example, the AI agents could make learning feedback and recommendations to complete learning tasks and provide a content flow bar tool for students to view the learning progress of what topics they have covered in the platform.

In addition to designing student-centered educational technologies, educators need to know the working principles behind an AI learning system such as how the recommendation systems suggest the learners to study or practice a specific content or how the automated scoring derives individualized comments and feedback. Otherwise, teachers and students would become passive and nonautonomous without gaining a transparent and comprehensive understanding of their inner workings. To open this black box of learning, Luckin (2017, p. 1) proposed that AI learning systems need information about: "(1) the learning curriculum, subject area and activities that each student is completing; (2) the details of the steps each student takes as they complete these activities; and (3) what counts a success within each of these activities and within each of the steps towards the completion of each activity." Another study Long and Magerko (2020) proposed the need to promote transparency of the AI design such as reducing black-boxed functionality, sharing creator intentions, and funding/data sources. In other words, the design of AI should reflect teacher and student intelligence with explainable reasoning and comprehensive understanding of what and why they receive the responses according to the AI agents' suggestions.

It is also important to note that there is unique human intelligence, such as creativity, socialization, design insights, and aspirations, which is hard, if not impossible, for AI to take over (e.g., Chen et al., 2022; Miller, 2019). Jain et al. (2021) builds on Shneiderman's (2020a, b) advocacy for HCAI that advances "fundamental human aspirations," such as expressing people's creative potentials, forming social connections, and promoting equity. Although human aspirations could be quantified in some sense through advancing the automatic recognition (e.g., visual complexity, colorfulness), teachers and students can use AI as tools to facilitate the representation and communication of abstract ideas and support their visual expression and reflective ideation.

9.3.3 Ethical and Responsible Design

Learning technologies with ethical and responsible design such as explainability, comprehensiveness, usefulness, and usability should be considered. Many educators show their worries that AI agents would replace their jobs and challenge the effectiveness of using AI to teach in their classrooms due to a number of concerns such as black-box machine learning, data bias (Rudin, 2019), trustworthiness, privacy (Reinhardt et al., 2022), and other ethical concerns (Toreini et al., 2020). Explainable AI enables teachers to understand the algorithm and the working principles behind. For example, learning analytics should provide reasons for students' grade prediction through AI-based assessments. The AI agents should offer transparent and trustworthy feedback to teachers, students, and parents about how the students learn, what type of support they need, and what is the progress they are making toward their learning goals (Luckin, 2017). The machine learning process and its working principles of AI learning technologies should be transparent and be visualized and explainable for all stakeholders of learning. Furthermore, comprehensive AI could adapt to students' needs and capabilities (e.g., knowledge level and learners' interest) to provide individualized feedback and make suitable teaching decisions. Useful AI means that AI should satisfy users' needs in a particular scenario of their work, study, and life. An example in the educational context, learners' behavioral patterns usage scenarios should be considered when modeling the users' learning needs and usage scenarios to make appropriate learners' reports. Usable AI indicates an effective HCI and user interface design that offer user experiences that specify users' requirements (Xu, 2019). Ipsita et al. (2022) designed a user-friendly interface that considers learners' behavioral modeling to offer graphical animations, display data for attributes of virtual reality objects, and manipulate with data and trigger controls in a mechanical engineering classroom. Big data and AI have a synergistic relationship that AI requires a massive scale of data to learn and improve decision-making processes. Therefore, instructional designers need to encourage students to investigate how data is generated and collected in their learning projects and the limitations and bias of the datasets (Long & Magerko, 2020).

9.3.4 AI Under Human Control and Under Human Conditions

Renz and Vladova (2021) further proposed the teaming ideas of education from two theoretical perspectives (i.e., AI under human control and AI under human conditions). The ideas are similar to Xu (2019) regarding the two perspectives. The former is subject to judgment based on the degree of human control over AI. In school settings, AI should be controllable and understood by users (e.g., school administrators, educators, students, parents) to support daily automation to improve educational administration and take control of their learning and teaching. The second idea "AI in the human condition" refers to the design of AI algorithms and working principles that should be explained, interpreted, and refined based on student learning needs, contexts, and phenomena.

Renz and Vladova (2021) also proposed the concept of "teaming" and suggested the importance of collaborating between users and AI agents. AI is an intelligent agent not only to perform administrative and learning tasks for users (teachers, parents, and students) but also to work with users as teaching assistants, learning facilitators, and moderators to build positive learning communities. We could find the coherence in other publications in our review that also raise the importance of vital roles, responsibilities, and characteristics of a collaborative AI agent. For example, Morrison (2021) followed the HCAI approach to develop AI learning companions to facilitate children who were born blind to experience social agency and develop the range of social attention skills to initiate and maintain their interactions and explore concepts learned incidentally through vision by using alternative perceptual modalities. Another study Pérez-Ortiz et al. (2021) designed a human-centered AI platform to provide learners with a number of educational tools to interact with open educational videos and tools to suit their pedagogical preferences of learners. Yang et al. (2021) proposed the importance of smart learning analytics and assessment that enables students to take control of their learning, know how they are performing compared to their peers, and help teachers to identify gaps in students' prerequisite knowledge and key skills.

With AI and HCAI knowledge, AI developers and educators could understand the individualized characteristics and needs of targeted learners so as to design positive human-centered AI-empowered learning environments, services, and designs that provide values to diversified learners, organizations, and society as a whole. Building on the consolidated domains and definition of HCAI, here we put forward a summary of five key domains of HCAI in education (see Table 9.1). Instructional designers can consider these factors to help design their curriculum, teaching tools, and platforms when implementing AI literacy education in their classrooms.

Table 9.1 A summary of HCAI in education

HCAI domains	HCAI in education
Human factors design	Instructional designers and teachers should consider the roles of AI when designing learning environments, tools, and technologies. A set of human factors design such as explainability, comprehensiveness, and transparency should be considered
Reflect human intelligence	AI reflects human intelligence (including teachers and students) which cannot be bypassed by AI and considers student-centered characteristics and needs (e.g., students' technical background, age, cultural background) in the AI-driven instructional design
Ethical and responsible design	AI should facilitate computational techniques that are both innovative and responsible. It needs to prioritize issues of fairness, accountability, transparency, and ethics as they relate to AI, ML, and NLP by drawing on fields with a sociotechnical orientation
AI under human control	AI should be controllable by users (e.g., administrators, teachers) to support daily administration and decision-making to facilitate their work A comprehensive reasoning of why the recipients (e.g., students, parents) receive the treatments should be given Other ethical concerns such as privacy, security, and safety were taken into account in the AI-driven learning systems
AI under human conditions	AI algorithms and working principles of the learning technologies that should be explained, interpreted, and refined according to students/users' needs and learning scenarios A feedback mechanism is necessary for developers to improve the systems and student learning conditions based on learner individualized needs

Printed in the United States
by Baker & Taylor Publisher Services